Employment Discrimination
An Employer's Guide

The information in this guide is being provided by the authors and publisher as a service to the business community. Although every effort has been made to ensure the accuracy and completeness of this information, the authors and publisher of this publication cannot be responsible for any errors or omissions, or any agency's interpretations, applications and changes of regulations described in this publication.

"This publication is designed to provide accurate and authoritative information in regard to the subject matter covered. It is sold with the understanding that the publisher is not engaged in rendering legal, accounting or other professional service. If legal advice or other expert assistance is required, the services of a competent person should be sought."

    —   *from a Declaration of Principles jointly adopted by a committee of the American Bar Association and a Committee of Publishers and Associations.*

Published by:
American Chamber of Commerce Publishers
5515 N. Cumberland Ave., Suite 815
Chicago, IL 60656
800-848-5645
www.hrsurvival.com

FRANCZEK SULLIVAN P.C.

FRANCZEK SULLIVAN P.C. is a Chicago-based law firm that represents management in all aspects of labor and employment law in both the private and public sectors. The firm was founded in 1994 by twelve partners from four highly regarded firms. The objectives in forming the firm were to provide top quality legal services with a practical perspective; to better control the costs of providing legal services through the use of technology and the sharing of experience; and to provide greater opportunities for professional growth. The twelve partners who formed the firm were immediately joined by 10 associates. Today the firm has grown to include 39 lawyers.

Franczek Sullivan stands among the premier labor, employment and education practices in the country. The Firm's clients include Fortune 100 companies and many small-to-medium size businesses and institutions. The Firm counsels, advises and represents clients across the United States from the largest and most complex cases to day-to-day consultation on more routine matters.

The firm's expertise extends to matters arising under the Labor Management Relations Act, the Civil Rights laws including Title VII, the Age Discrimination in Employment Act and the Americans with Disabilities Act, the Occupational Safety and Health Act, the laws regulating employee pensions and other benefits (ERISA and related laws), the Family Medical Leave Act, the Worker Adjustment, Reemployment and Notification Act, the Railway Labor Act, state employment laws, labor contract negotiation and arbitration, due-diligence investigations of labor and employment law compliance, public sector civil rights laws, and employment litigation in all courts and agencies. In addition to its labor and employment practice, the firm also concentrates in the area of school law. The firm's attorneys are active in local, state and national bar associations and frequently speak to professional management groups on topics of interest in the labor and employment field. Several of the firm's lawyers are adjunct instructors in employment law.

FRANCZEK SULLIVAN P.C.
300 South Wacker Drive, Suite 3400
Chicago, Illinois 60606
(312) 986-0300
(312) 986-9192 (Facsimile)
www.nlfpc.com

For further information, including
fee schedules and lawyer profiles, contact:
Jacquelyn L. Golab
Director of Administration
(312) 786-6186

About the Editors

Sally J. Scott is a graduate of the University of Michigan School of Law. Throughout her legal career, Ms. Scott has concentrated exclusively on the practice of labor and employment law. She represents public and private sector employers in all areas of labor, employment and discrimination law, with a special concentration in occupational safety and health law. She regularly speaks to employers and employer associations and has authored numerous articles on employment law issues.

Thomas Koutsouvas is a graduate of the George Washington University Law School. He represents public and private sector clients in numerous areas of labor and employment law, including matters before state and federal courts, and various administrative agencies. Mr. Koutsouvas' work in these areas involves counseling and litigation on employment discrimination laws such as Title VII of the Civil Rights Act, the Americans with Disabilities Act and the Age Discrimination in Employment Act. He also represents employers on traditional union matters such as unfair labor practice claims and collective bargaining issues.

Susan E. Provenzano is a graduate of the University of Wisconsin Law School. She represents private and public sector employers in all areas of labor law, including employment litigation, ERISA litigation and union-related matters. She has handled arbitrations and matters before state and federal courts and administrative agencies involving employment discrimination under Title VII, the ADA and the ADEA, ERISA, wrongful termination, noncompetition agreements and labor practices. Ms. Provenzano has also drafted petitions for certiorari to the United States Supreme Court and appellate briefs to federal circuit courts of appeal on a variety of employment law issues.

Principal Authors

Stephanie A. Beauregard

Shelli L. Boyer

Michael A. Cox

Erika Dillon

Leah D. Gidron

Julie Heuberger

Gregory Isbell

Catherine E. Kearney

Lisa A. Lopatka

Timothy P. McGrory

Jeremy C. Moritz

Jennifer Schilling

Anne Wilson Lokken

Introduction

Laws regulating discriminatory employment actions are political responses to arbitrary management practices. In general, these laws prohibit policies and actions that have little, if any, business justification. Some employers have incurred liability for violating employment discrimination laws simply because they acted out of impatience or passing frustration without first thoughtfully assessing the business implications of their actions or giving the affected employees opportunities for comment. Other employers have incurred liability by delegating important personnel decisions to insufficiently trained subordinates, or by failing carefully to document performance deficiencies or differences that form the bases for actions. Sometimes, employers suffer liability solely because of careless or thoughtless comments that have no bearing on a disputed decision, but are given great significance by juries anxious to make statements against employers in general.

The reality is that these anti-discrimination laws, however numerous and superficially complex they might seem, do not, in fact, prevent management from conducting business efficiently and profitably. These laws do not prohibit consideration of ability or experience, accomplishments, academic credentials, or other positive attributes as bases for employment decisions. Management is not prohibited from making judgments about employee contributions to the business, even when those judgments are mistaken. These laws respect management decisions concerning allocations of capital, decisions to go into and get out of lines of business, implementation of work rules, production standards, and safety standards, pricing of products and services, quality control, customer relations and virtually every other management function that is required for a successful business enterprise. There may at times be need for some added expenditures as when an individual with a disability requires a ramp to access the employment office, or when an employee's job must be kept open while she is taking short-term family leave. However, any employer who has worked through these situations will attest that these costs are manageable and may be offset by increased productivity and employee morale. In any case, the anti-discrimination laws are fixtures that must be understood by employers at the risk of incurring significant liabilities and the costs and displacements of litigation. These laws must be made the subject of managed compliance planning.

The purpose of this manual is to help employers manage their workforces more efficiently and profitably through a better understanding of the relatively limited range of prohibitions the employment discrimination laws actually present. The manual is intended to identify certain kinds of actions or inactions that may require particular documentation, more thoughtful consideration, or pre-planning, in order to avoid even the appearance of arbitrariness that can lead to charges of illegal discrimination and litigation that will be expensive, time consuming and disruptive regardless of the outcome. As experienced management-side employment lawyers, the authors of this manual wish to communicate the idea that the employment discrimination laws need not pose a significant barrier to a successful business enterprise. We hope to show why that is so through the law-by-law analysis and pointers that follow.

We welcome your comments, experiences and reactions.

Robert E. Mann

Franczek Sullivan, P.C.
300 South Wacker Drive
Chicago, Illinois 60606
(312) 986-0300
(312) 986-9192 (Facsimile)
Web Site   http://www.nlfpc.com

Chapter table
of contents

Table of contents

Chapter 5

Resolving employee disputes/charges 29

Chapter 6

Race discrimination 35

Chapter 7
National origin discrimination 45

Chapter 8
Religious discrimination. 51

Chapter 9
Sex discrimination 59

Chapter 10

Sexual harassment 67

Chapter 11

Age discrimination 79

Chapter 12
Disability discrimination. 87

Chapter 16
Military status discrimination. 129

Chapter 17
Discrimination in employee benefits. 137

Chapter 21

Discrimination prohibited by state law . . . 171

Chapter 22

Discrimination based on credit history . . . 191

Chapter 1

Snapshot

Employers are not allowed to make employment decisions on the basis of personal characteristics that are defined by law. These include race, skin color, national origin, religious belief, age (if in excess of 40 years), gender, disability (if the employee is able to perform essential functions with or without reasonable accommodation), characteristics protected by various state laws (for example, sexual orientation), and the right to protest employment actions based on these characteristics. Most employers do not make or intend to make employment decisions on the basis of these characteristics. Nevertheless, each year a large number of these employers become involved in expensive litigation with uncertain outcomes and potentially costly settlements, not because they knowingly committed illegal acts but, rather, simply because they failed beforehand to install an effective compliance program.

This checklist of the laws will help you to determine whether your compliance program needs attention. A "no" answer to any of the questions does not necessarily indicate non-compliance, but should put you on notice of a potential trouble area.

The page number is provided for quick reference.

Yes	No		Page reference
❏	❏	Are all notices and posters required by law to provide information to employees posted in a place where employees easily can read them?	*
❏	❏	Does your company have a policy against employment discrimination?	16
○	○	Does the company's policy specifically identify a management person (not merely an office, but an actual person) to whom questions and complaints may be submitted?	
○	○	Does that management person have the authority to take effective action to investigate complaints and to take effective remedial action in case of policy violations?	
○	○	Are employees made aware of that manager's authority?	

* – See companion **Survival Guide**.

			Page reference
Yes	**No**		
O	O	Does that manager have access to competent legal advice regarding compliance issues?	
O	O	Is the manager aware of the risks of libel claims from persons falsely accused of unlawful discrimination and does he or she know how to avoid such claims?	
O	O	Does the company's policy specifically identify a management person to handle requests for job accommodations?	
O	O	Does the company have written job descriptions?	
O	O	Are these descriptions reviewed and updated regularly to ensure they list essential job functions?	
❏	❏	Have all personnel who are in a position to make, or to recommend, decisions about hiring, training, job assignment, evaluation, disciplinary actions, discharge, leave request approval, content of jobs, layoffs, benefits administration and other employment actions been instructed not to make decisions or recommendations based on employees' protected statuses?	9
❏	❏	Does the company have a policy against harassment?	75
O	O	Is the policy written, signed and dated by a current top management person?	
O	O	Is the policy posted where it can be read by all employees?	
O	O	Does the policy have a complaint procedure?	
O	O	Does the policy identify more than one management person to whom complaints can be reported?	
O	O	Does the policy include the consequences for violations?	
O	O	Have all personnel been instructed about the policy, the conduct that will violate the policy, the consequences of violation, the steps an employee may take to make a complaint, and the right to be protected from discrimination or retaliation because of submitting a complaint?	

Yes	No		Page reference
❏	❏	Does the company issue an employee handbook or manual that describes company policies?	157
○	○	Has the handbook or manual been examined within the past year to determine whether the statements made in it are legal and express current company policy?	
❏	❏	Does the company have government contracts?	151
○	○	If so, does the company have an affirmative action plan?	
○	○	Does the affirmative action plan make realistic evaluations of differences (if any) between the company's employment of minorities and females and the availability of minorities and females for jobs with the firm?	
○	○	Has the plan been updated within the past year by a person who understands what the government auditors expect?	
❏	❏	Is there a program to track the hiring, job assignment, promotion and discharge processes to determine whether these processes include unintended negative effects based on protected factors?	11
○	○	Has someone investigated to determine whether the laws of the state(s) in which your company employs persons prohibit employment discrimination on the basis of protected statuses other than race, gender, national origin, religion, age and disability?	
❏	❏	Is there a person specially assigned to review leave requests?	112
○	○	Has that person received training about the rights and responsibilities of employees and the company under the Family and Medical Leave Act and any applicable state laws that may apply?	
❏	❏	Is the medical expense indemnity plan that your company provides in compliance with changes in laws concerning discrimination against persons with particular conditions such as AIDS/HIV?	145

Compliance thresholds

The following list does not include all discrimination laws, but it does provide the most significant laws and how many employees an employer must have to be covered. Remember, however, that coverage for some of the laws also depends upon requirements other than the number of employees. If the number places your business on the borderline, consult the chapter provided for an explanation of those other requirements. See Chapter 2, **Compliance thresholds**, in the companion **Survival Guide** for a listing of general employment laws.

Minimum employees	Law	Notes		Chapter
0	Executive Order 11246	Federal contractors	6	**Race discrimination**
			18	**Affirmative action**
0	Rehabilitation Act of 1973	Federal contractors	12	**Disability discrimination**
0	The Vietnam Era Veterans' Readjustment Assistance Act of 1974	Federal contractors	16	**Military status discrimination**
			18	**Affirmative action**
1	The Civil Rights Act of 1866, Section 1981		7	**National origin discrimination**
			6	**Race discrimination**
1	Consumer Credit Protection Act		22	**Discrimination based on credit history**

Minimum employees	Law	Notes	Chapter
1	Employee Retirement Income Security Act	17	**Discrimination in employee benefits**
1	The Fair Credit Reporting Act	22	**Discrimination based on credit history**
1	National Labor Relations Act, Section 7	14	**Protection of employee organizational and union activities**
1	Occupational Safety and Health Act	15	**Discrimination based on safety activities**
1	The Uniform Services Employment & Reemployment Rights Act of 1994	16	**Military status discrimination**
2	Equal Pay Act (Fair Labor Standards Act)	9	**Sex discrimination**
15	Americans with Disabilities Act	12	**Disability discrimination**
		9	**Sex discrimination**
		17	**Discrimination in employee benefits**
15	Pregnancy Discrimination Act of 1978	9	**Sex discrimination**

Minimum employees	Law	Notes		Chapter
15	Title VII of the Civil Rights Act of 1964		7	**National origin discrimination**
			6	**Race discrimination**
			8	**Religious discrimination**
			9	**Sex discrimination**
20	Age Discrimination in Employment Act		11	**Age discrimination**
			17	**Discrimination in employee benefits**
20	Older Workers Benefit Protection Act of 1990		11	**Age discrimination**
50	Family and Medical Leave Act of 1993		9	**Sex discrimination**
			13	**Family and Medical Leave Act**

Chapter 3

Discrimination in a nutshell

An employer violates anti-discrimination laws when it bases an adverse employment decision on an employee's or applicant's protected status or protected conduct. It is not unlawful, generally speaking, to base an employment decision on an employee's or applicant's education, experience, skill, work performance, or employment history.

What is protected status

Protected status is a characteristic that employers are prohibited from considering in making employment decisions. Federal law protects the following characteristics:

- **Race** (Chapter 6)
  Employers may not base employment decisions on an employee's or applicant's race or stereotypes associated with race. An increasing number of claims are being made that an employer has discriminated against an employee or applicant because he or she is Caucasian (reverse discrimination claims).

- **National origin** (Chapter 7)
  It is unlawful to consider an employee's national origin in making employment decisions. An English language requirement may be challenged as discriminatory if it is not a required part of the job.

- **Religion (both beliefs and practices)** (Chapter 8)
  Not only is an employer prohibited from discriminating against employees because of their religious beliefs, but also an employer has a duty to reasonably accommodate religious practices. For example, an employer who grants time off for Judeo-Christian holidays may have a duty to grant time off for employees of other religions on their holy days.

- **Sex or gender** (Chapters 9 and 10)
  Sexual harassment and pregnancy discrimination are forms of sex or gender discrimination. Same-sex harassment is also an unlawful form of discrimination.

- **Age (40 years of age or older)** (Chapter 11)
  The replacement of an employee over 40 years of age with a "substantially younger" employee may create a suspicion of age discrimination, even if the replacement employee was also over 40.

- **Disability (physical and mental)** (Chapter 12)
  Employers are not only prohibited from unlawfully discriminating against persons with disabilities, but they also may have a duty to modify a disabled employee's non-essential job functions if necessary to allow the employee to perform his or her job.

- **Military status (current and former)** (Chapter 16)
  An employer must grant employees in the national guard or military reserves up to five years of leave for the purposes of fulfilling their military duties.

- **Marital status** (Chapter 13)
  Most state laws prohibit discrimination against employees because they are married.

- **Sexual orientation** (Chapter 10)
  Federal law currently does not recognize sexual orientation as a protected status. However, some state and local laws specifically prohibit discrimination based on sexual orientation.

- **Arrest and conviction records** (Chapter 21)
  Basing employment decisions on an applicant's criminal history is not directly prohibited by federal law, but it may be discriminatory if such a practice is not justified by business necessity and has a direct impact on a protected group (see page 36, **Disparate impact claims**). Some states also specifically prohibit employers from relying on criminal records in making employment decisions.

- **Off-the-job lawful use of products** (Chapter 21)
  Although many state laws and local ordinances now prohibit smoking in places of employment, some states protect the right of an employee to engage in activities, such as smoking, while off duty.

What is protected conduct

Employers are prohibited from retaliating against an employee or applicant for engaging in protected conduct; that is, exercising rights guaranteed by law. Examples of protected conduct include:

- Filing an internal sexual harassment complaint against another employee, so long as the complaining party has a good-faith basis for the complaint.

- Filing a charge of discrimination with the Equal Employment Opportunity Commission or lawsuit in court or assisting another employee in doing so.

- Requesting a reasonable accommodation of a disability or religious practice.

- Requesting family or medical leave under the Family and Medical Leave Act or military leave under the Uniformed Services Employment and Reemployment Rights Act.

- Voicing a concern that an employment decision (either affecting the employee voicing the concern or another employee) was based on a protected characteristic.

- Reporting an unsafe condition to the Occupational Safety and Health Administration.

Typical discrimination situations

Adverse employment decisions can subject an employer to liability under the anti-discrimination laws, if an employee or applicant can prove that the decision was based on his or her protected status or protected conduct. Examples of adverse employment decisions include:

- Failure to hire, train or promote

- Demotion or discipline

- Layoff or discharge

- Salary freeze

- Unequal pay or benefits for employees performing the same or similar work

- Failure to grant a request for a reasonable accommodation of a disability or religious practice

- Harassment by managers or by co-workers

- Constructive discharge
  Courts sometimes treat an employee who has resigned as if he or she has been discharged, if the employee can prove that his or her working life was made so miserable by the employer that any reasonable person in his or her position would have felt compelled to resign. For example, a C.E.O. who resigns after she is demoted to junior clerk and is made to do routine filing may be able to show that she was constructively discharged.

Different types of unlawful discrimination

Four basic types of unlawful discrimination include:

1. Disparate treatment

2. Disparate impact

3. Harassment

4. Undertaking or failing to undertake certain actions prohibited or required by law.

1. **Disparate treatment**

Disparate treatment is treating an employee or applicant differently than others who are similarly situated because of the employee's/applicant's protected status or protected conduct. For example, it may be discriminatory to discipline an African-American office assistant who has accumulated three unexcused absences if a Caucasian office assistant with equivalent absenteeism was not disciplined, unless there is a legitimate reason for the difference in treatment (for example, the African-American office assistant also is guilty of insubordination). Most claims of discrimination are of this type.

An employee or applicant who claims to have been discriminated against will win his or her case if the employee can show, with direct or circumstantial evidence, that it is more likely than not that his or her protected status or conduct was a factor motivating an adverse employment decision.

- Direct evidence is an acknowledgment of discriminatory intent. For example, stating in a memorandum from the decision-maker to an employee's boss that the employee is being discharged because the employee "is too old for this line of work." This type of evidence is very rare.

- Circumstantial evidence is evidence from which one can fairly draw an inference of discriminatory intent. There are 3 types of circumstantial evidence:

    1. "bits and pieces" evidence such as:

        - suspicious timing (for example, discharge within days of a complaint of sexual harassment)

        - ambiguous written or oral statements (for example, in reference to a female employee with children, the statement that "women at her stage in life are always out the door at ten minutes to five")

        - behavior toward or comments directed at other employees in the protected group (for example, repeated references to adult female employees as "girls," "honeys," or "sweethearts").

    2. "comparative" evidence that employees who do not share the protected status received better treatment (for example, a female employee fired for theft may show that male employees accused of the same or similar offense were only suspended).

3. "pretext" evidence that the employer's stated reason for the adverse employment decision is a lie (for example, an employee whom the employer claims was fired due to a reduction-in-force may show that the employer actually was adding staff in the fired employee's classification at the time of the discharge).

An employer that has engaged in discrimination or retaliation may be able to avoid an award of damages by proving that it would have taken the same adverse action against the employee in any event, even absent the employee's protected status or conduct. This is called a "mixed-motive" defense.

2. Disparate impact

Disparate impact discrimination occurs when a neutral employment policy or practice disproportionately impacts persons with a particular protected status and there is no solid business justification for the policy or practice. For example, it may be discriminatory to require all applicants for a dockworker position to be able to lift 100 pounds to shoulder height if, on the job, employees are required to lift boxes weighing only up to 60 pounds and the lifting requirement disproportionately screens out women or persons with disabilities. On the other hand, if employees are regularly required to lift boxes weighing at least 100 pounds, the lifting requirement probably is not discriminatory, despite its impact on women and certain disabled individuals. That is because there is a business justification for the requirement.

An employer may be found liable for discrimination under a disparate impact theory even if there is no evidence that the challenged practice was intended to discriminate against a protected class. Disparate impact may be proven by evidence that a challenged hiring practice results in a statistically significant difference between the composition of the employer's workforce and the composition of qualified individuals in the workforce generally. For example, disparate impact may be found where an employer's hiring criteria caused its workforce to include only a small percentage of women, even though statistics show that qualified women are widely available in the local community. Unlawful discrimination will be found if there is no business justification for the criteria that screens out women.

3. Harassment

Harassment based on a protected status is a form of discrimination. Although sexual harassment is the most common and widely discussed type of harassment, discrimination laws prohibit harassment based on other protected statuses, such as race and national origin. See page 9 for a definition of **Protected status**.

Responsibility for supervisors

Under the Supreme Court's 1998 decisions in <u>Faragher v. Boca Raton</u> and <u>Burlington v. Ellerth</u>, employers are **automatically** liable for sexual harassment where a supervisor makes submission to sexual advances an implicit or explicit condition for receiving a tangible job benefit (such as a promotion or raise), or avoiding a tangible job detriment (such as a demotion or discharge). Where the supervisor merely threatens certain actions and/or engages in behavior that creates a hostile environment, the employer is liable unless it can prove both that:

- it has a policy against sexual harassment which is distributed to employees and enforced

  and

- the employee complaining of the harassment acted unreasonably by not using the complaint procedure in the policy.

Although the Supreme Court's cases addressed sexual harassment, lower courts are applying the same test to other forms of harassment, such as racial harassment, committed by supervisors or managers.

Responsibility for employees

An employer is liable for harassment by one co-worker against another that occurs in the workplace if the employer knew or should have known about the co-worker's conduct and failed to take appropriate remedial action. Therefore, even if an employee has been harassed, an employer may prevail against a claim of harassment by one employee against another, if as soon as it learns of the harassment, it takes adequate remedial action reasonably calculated to prevent further harassment.

4. Failing to undertake certain actions

Failing to undertake certain actions required by law may also violate anti-discrimination laws Examples of such actions are:

- Failing to reasonably accommodate a known disability of an employee or applicant.

- Failing to reasonably accommodate an employee's religious practices, for example, refusing to permit a Muslim employee to pray at required times during the workday.

Practical pointers

- **Consistently document performance or disciplinary problems and discuss them with employees at the time they occur.**
  An employee who is informed of deficiencies as they come to light and given an opportunity to improve will be less likely and less able to claim later on that an adverse employment action was based on protected status or conduct. Document the deficiencies and the communication to the employee. While it is important to document, do not "over document" every incident, if the same process is not followed with other employees.

- **Tell employees the true reasons for the Company's adverse actions.**
  For instance, if an employee is terminated for poor performance, do not spare the employee's feelings by stating that it was due to a "downsizing." Anything less than complete candor, even if well-intentioned, may be used as evidence that the reason given to the employee was a "pretext" for discrimination.

- **Maintain and enforce a strict anti-discrimination and anti-harassment policy.**
  An effective anti-harassment policy can limit an employer's potential liability for harassment or discrimination committed by supervisors or employees in many situations. This policy should contain a complaint procedure that gives employees options as to whom to make their complaint. For example, it should not require employees to report the harassment to their immediate supervisors. An employee's immediate supervisor may be the wrongdoer. Employees might be provided the option of reporting the harassment to their department head or the Human Resources Director, for example. The policy should encourage employees to report harassment immediately, before it becomes severe. This will allow the employer to correct the situation before harassment becomes severe enough to expose the employer to liability. The policy also should assure employees that they will not be retaliated against for utilizing the complaint procedure.

- **Review all personnel decisions to reduce the likelihood that an employment decision is the result of an unlawful bias held by a supervisor or manager.**
  The employer should develop institutional "checks" on supervisory authority, such as requiring that all hiring, discharge or promotions be approved by at least two management representatives.

- **Use job-related criteria to screen potential applicants; do not rely on criteria that have no bearing on job performance.**
  For example, for a manual labor job, do not screen applicants based on whether they have a high school diploma. Conversely, do not use a physical agility test to screen applicants for a desk job.

Chapter 4

Anatomy of a discrimination charge and lawsuit

Laws prohibiting employment discrimination are enforced by a combination of local, state and federal administrative agencies and courts. In general, a claim of discrimination begins with the filing of a discrimination charge with an administrative agency. The agency then is given an opportunity to investigate the charge and attempt to resolve the dispute between the employee and employer. If the charge is not resolved, the employee may then sue the employer in federal court or in a special administrative tribunal established at the state level. In some cases, the administrative agency may file suit in court on behalf of employees. This chapter provides an overview of agency and court procedures.

What is the role of regulatory agencies?

Anti-discrimination laws are enforced by various regulatory agencies at the federal, state, and local level. These agencies do 3 things:

1. Receive and investigate charges

2. Issue compliance guidelines and regulations

3. Bring discrimination lawsuits in court on behalf of employees (at the federal level), or provide a forum for litigating employment discrimination disputes (state level).

The EEOC has primary responsibility for enforcing federal employment discrimination laws. Most states and many local governmental bodies have agencies, often called Fair Employment Practices, Civil Rights, or Department of Human Rights that investigate alleged violations of state and local anti-discrimination laws and ordinances.

Usually, an employee first must file a charge of discrimination first with the EEOC or a state agency before he or she may file a lawsuit in court. The agencies are legally obligated to accept a properly completed charge, regardless of its merit.

Deadlines for filing a charge of discrimination

A charge of discrimination must be filed:

- with either the EEOC or applicable state agency within 300 days of the alleged act of discrimination

  or

- in states with no local agency, a charge must be filed with the EEOC within 180 days of the alleged act of discrimination.

Overview of EEOC procedures

The EEOC will send a properly filed charge to the employer along with a form letter requesting that the employer respond to the charge by filing a statement explaining the employer's position by a specified date. An employer should fully investigate the charge before filing a position statement. Untrue or inaccurate statements contained in a position statement may be used against the employer as evidence that the employer is attempting to cover up discrimination actions. Chapter 19, **Management of discrimination charges**, contains detailed guidance on investigating and responding to discrimination charges.

How the EEOC determines which charges merit investigation

To reduce backlog and focus administrative resources on priority cases, the EEOC is now classifying each charge as follows:

- **Category A**
  Further investigation is likely to result in a finding of discrimination: Charge will receive priority treatment and will be investigated further.

- **Category B**
  It is unclear whether further investigation will result in a finding of discrimination: Charge will be investigated as agency resources permit.

- **Category C**
  It is unlikely that further investigation will disclose a violation: Charge will be dismissed without further investigation.

These administrative changes recognize that the EEOC simply does not have sufficient resources to investigate every charge that is filed and place substantial decision-making authority in field offices and with front-line investigators and attorneys. The EEOC will not disclose its categorization of a charge. However, the employer, through its position statement and conversations with the investigator, should appeal to the discretion of these front-line people and attempt to persuade them that the charge does not merit the diversion of the agency's resources.

How the EEOC investigates a charge

The questionnaire

The EEOC, or its state agency counterpart, may send out a questionnaire that asks the employer to answer written questions and produce documents. Such requests often use a standard form and are not tailored to the specific issue raised by the charge. The employer should approach such requests with common sense. The employer should not simply provide raw information. Rather, careful thought should be given to answering questions in a manner that explains why the information provided supports the employer's position. Also, the employer should not necessarily provide information simply because it is asked, at least initially. The EEOC has the authority to issue a subpoena compelling the production of requested information, and courts generally will enforce such requests. However, remember that the EEOC's resources are limited, and it will not issue a subpoena unless it believes the information is necessary and informal efforts at obtaining the information have failed.

Key point

Providing information is like opening up Pandora's Box. Once information is disclosed, it cannot be retracted. However, an employer can always supplement its questionnaire response or provide additional information later on if asked to do so. More detailed guidance on how to respond to an agency questionnaire can be found in Chapter 19, **Management of discrimination charges**.

The fact-finding conference

The EEOC, or its state agency counterpart, will sometimes conduct a fact-finding conference, which is an informal, face-to-face meeting moderated by the agency investigator between the charging party and an employer representative with knowledge of the relevant facts. In recent years, the EEOC has not extensively used such conferences, but many state agencies continue to use them. At the fact-finding investigation, the investigator will question each party regarding their respective positions and may attempt to broker a settlement of the charge. The employer and employee may bring attorneys to advise them; however, it is the employee and employer representatives who must answer the questions asked by the investigator.

The on-site investigation

An on-site investigation is similar to a fact-finding conference but it occurs on the employer's premises and the complainant is not present. In recent years the EEOC has preferred to use on-site investigations rather than fact-finding conferences. The investigator may want to question employees outside the presence of management personnel or the employer's attorney. Employers have objected successfully to the questioning of management personnel (those with decision making authority in personnel matters), without an attorney present as potentially violating the attorney-client privilege. However, objecting to the interview of non-management employees may be viewed as obstructionist and is unlikely to be successful (the investigator will simply find other ways to contact them). The EEOC must give reasonable notice of any investigation, and it must conduct the investigation in a manner that does not unduly disrupt the employer's business. The best way to control the scope of the investigation and minimize any disruption is to determine from the investigator in advance the anticipated length of the investigation, whom the investigator wants to question, and what the investigator wants to see.

Key point
Be cooperative and reasonable, but don't give the investigator free reign of the facility. See Chapter 19, **Management of discrimination charges**, for additional information.

After the EEOC investigation

The EEOC has no authority to issue awards. It also has no authority to clear an employer of any wrongdoing. At the conclusion of its investigation, the EEOC must decide whether to file suit in federal court on the employee's behalf or to dismiss the charge and allow the employee to sue on his or her own behalf. In most cases the EEOC simply will dismiss the charge and issue a "notice of right to sue" to the employee. The employee then has 90 days to file suit in federal court.

The "notice of right to sue" may or may not be accompanied by a specific finding by the EEOC as to whether it suspects discrimination occurred. The EEOC dismisses many charges without making any finding as to whether discrimination is suspected. Because an EEOC investigation may take years to complete, it is becoming increasingly common for a complaining party to ask the EEOC to dismiss a charge, so the complaining party may sue in federal court.

There currently is a conflict among the federal appellate courts as to the legality of the EEOC's practice of dismissing charges without conducting an independent investigation. Some courts, including the federal appellate court for the District of Columbia have held that the EEOC's dismissal of a charge without conducting an independent investigation violates Title VII of the Civil Rights Act, which both requires the EEOC to investigate all charges and prohibits the EEOC from issuing a notice of right to sue letter until after a charge has been pending at least 180 days. By contrast, the Ninth and Eleventh Circuits have held that the EEOC does have the authority under Title VII to dismiss charges within 180 days when it is unlikely to complete its investigation within that time period.

When the EEOC will sue an employer

The EEOC receives many more charges than it can prosecute itself, therefore it has adopted a National Enforcement Plan that identifies the type of cases that the EEOC intends to litigate itself.

The EEOC's National Enforcement Plan identifies 3 types of cases that the EEOC intends to litigate itself:

- cases that will have an impact beyond the parties in the particular dispute (such as instances of repeated and/or flagrant violations, or cases challenging broad based employment practices within an industry).

- cases that would promote the development of the law in the area of employment discrimination (such as cases that involve an unresolved issue of a law or regulation interpretation, particularly those under the Americans with Disabilities Act, a relatively new statute).

- cases involving the integrity or the effectiveness of the EEOC enforcement process (such as cases dealing with the scope of the EEOC's subpoena power).

Some discrimination charges filed by employees clearly are frivolous and may be effectively handled by an experienced human resources professional. However, if an employer receives a "Commissioner's Charge" filed by an EEOC Commissioner it means that the EEOC has earmarked the matter for priority treatment and an attorney should be consulted immediately.

Steps the EEOC will take to settle a charge

Many discrimination charges are settled before the EEOC completes an investigation. The investigator often will attempt to act as an informal mediator in order to facilitate a settlement and sometimes can be an employer's ally in dealing with an unreasonable employee. The EEOC has also recently adopted a more formalized mediation program that utilizes independent mediators. Under the EEOC's proposed plan for the use of alternative dispute resolution, all Category A and B charges (see page 18, **Category A** and **Category B**) will be eligible for mediation (subject to the EEOC's discretion to remove certain cases from eligibility, such as those that fit within the criteria of the National Enforcement Plan identified above). Voluntary mediation is to be offered to the parties before any further investigation has occurred. If mediation is unsuccessful the charging party may request a right to sue letter. Otherwise, the charge will be processed following normal procedures.

At the conclusion of its investigation, the EEOC may attempt to engage in settlement discussions, which the agency refers to as "conciliation." If so, the EEOC will act as a conciliator, attempting to negotiate a settlement between the parties. Even in instances where the EEOC's investigation has disclosed possible unlawful discrimination, the agency will typically encourage the parties to resolve their dispute if the settlement grants substantial, or something less than full, relief to the complaining party. For Category C charges, the EEOC will usually dismiss the charges without attempting to negotiate a settlement.

EEOC guidelines on use of waivers

Employers frequently include waivers of the right to file discrimination charges in employment documents such as separation agreements and settlement agreements. However, in its Guidance on Waivers Under Civil Rights Laws, the EEOC asserts that an employer cannot interfere with an employee's right to file charges of discrimination under federal civil rights laws. Further, an employer cannot interfere with an employee's right to "testify, assist, or participate in any manner" involving an EEOC proceeding.

The EEOC contends that any agreements "extracting . . . promises" not to file a charge or appear in an EEOC proceeding will be "null and void as a matter of public policy" and "may amount to separate and discrete violations of anti-retaliation provisions" covered by these anti-discrimination laws. According to the Guidance, employee waivers "deprive" the EEOC of important testimony and other evidence necessary to determine whether employers have violated employment discrimination laws. Citing to the public interest in eliminating unlawful employment discrimination, the EEOC notes that waivers have a chilling effect on an employee's willingness and ability to come forward with information regarding discrimination claims.

How state agencies differ from the EEOC

Most states, and many larger municipalities, have their own agencies that enforce state and local anti-discrimination laws. The EEOC has entered into work sharing agreements with these state agencies in an attempt to avoid duplication of effort between the EEOC and the local agency. Under these agreements, a charge that is filed with the state agency is automatically "dual filed" with the EEOC and "vice versa;" and only one of the agencies will conduct an investigation. The EEOC gives "substantial weight" to the investigation results of a state agency, which means that it is not bound by the state agency's decision, but usually will follow it.

Most states have adopted procedures for charge filing, fact finding, and conciliation similar to those used by the EEOC. However, unlike federal law, once the agency investigation is completed, enforcement proceedings usually are conducted through an administrative tribunal, rather than by filing suit in court. These proceedings consist of a hearing before a hearing officer similar to a court proceeding, but usually less formal. The hearing officer's determination generally is then reviewed by a panel of commissioners. The final decision of the state agency is subject to appellate review by a state court.

Some states do not require charges to be filed first with an administrative agency, but permit an employee to file suit directly in state court.

Who decides where a charge will be brought

An employee usually will have a choice of a federal or state forum. Not surprisingly, an employee and his or her attorney usually will choose the most favorable forum to their position. State and federal law may differ with respect to applicable statutes of limitations, permissible remedies, and jurisdictional requirements. Moreover, even where the law is substantially the same, some state tribunals may be perceived as more "employee friendly" than their federal counterparts, or vice versa. For instance, in the 1980's, there was a perception that many Reagan appointed federal judges were pro-employer, resulting in an influx of cases at the state level. Today, in states where employment discrimination claims are resolved through an administrative hearing, not a jury trial, many employees and their attorneys will maneuver to get a case to federal court, where jury trials are now available.

Because discrimination charges are "dual filed" at both the EEOC and state agency, the place where a charge is filed initially does not necessarily determine where litigation occurs. A charging party whose claim is investigated by the state agency may request the right to sue in federal court from the EEOC. The state agency will then terminate its investigation. However, if the state agency, following an investigation, decides to bring a claim against the employer on behalf of an employee, it will do so in the state administrative tribunal, or in state court, whichever is applicable.

An overview of court procedures

An employer may be sued in federal court by either the EEOC or an employee who has received a right to sue notice from the EEOC. The vast majority of employment discrimination cases are brought by individuals represented by private attorneys after receiving a "notice of right to sue." Although certain aspects of litigation may differ according to the specific facts of each case, most cases share the following procedural similarities.

Discovery

Unless the employer can convince the judge to dismiss the case because the employee cannot legally prevail on a lawsuit even if all the facts alleged in the complaint are true, the case will proceed to discovery. Discovery consists of the exchange of information between parties through the production of documentary evidence, responding to written questions (called interrogatories), and the taking of depositions. In an employment case, the crucial issue is the motive of the person who made the employment decision in dispute. Therefore, extensive discovery will usually be to the employee's benefit because it is the employer that has most of the information bearing on the reasons for its actions.

The employee's attorney usually will take the depositions of people involved in the employment decision. The importance of cooperating with company attorneys and preparing thoroughly in advance for depositions cannot be over-stressed. At a deposition, the decision makers will be asked to justify their decisions. A finding of discrimination may be based on nothing more than the inability of an employer's witnesses to persuasively explain the reasons for perfectly legitimate actions, or key inconsistencies between witness testimony. **No witness, no matter how experienced speaking "off the cuff" in business situations, should presume that he can bluff his way through the deposition process without adequate preparation.**

The employer's discovery will focus primarily on the deposition of the employee, because there the employer may ask the employee directly to explain, in his or her own words, why the employee believes he or she has been the victim of discrimination.

Summary judgment motion

A summary judgment motion asks the court to dispose of the case short of trial based on the facts uncovered in discovery. An employer can obtain summary judgment if it can convince the judge that even if a jury accepts every relevant fact asserted by the employee as true, those facts do not prove discrimination. Summary judgment is important because:

- it gives an employer an opportunity to avoid a trial, an inherently risky and expensive proposition

- it forces employees to put forward evidence that would permit a finding of discrimination, not mere unfairness. Employees sue because they believe, rightly or wrongly, that they have been treated unfairly. The law recognizes, however, that employees' subjective belief that they have been treated unfairly is not discrimination.

Jury trials

With the passage of the Civil Rights Act of 1991, jury trials are now available for claims of intentional discrimination. Whenever an employer makes a decision that may be challenged in a court of law, the employer should recognize that the matter may some day end up before a jury. Employers should remember the following about jury trials.

- They are difficult for employers to win because most jurors sympathize with individuals, not corporations or government entities.

- The jury is likely to base its decision on whether the employee was treated fairly, not whether the employee was a victim of discrimination.

- They are expensive to litigate.

- Media reports of large verdicts in discrimination cases have raised expectations of both plaintiff's attorneys and their clients, making cases more difficult/expensive to settle.

Potential employer liabilities

The remedies available to a plaintiff who proves discrimination in federal court depend on the specific facts of each claim. A plaintiff that proves unlawful discrimination at trial generally may be entitled to the following remedies.

Backpay

The amount of earnings and benefits the employee would have earned had he or she not been discharged, demoted etc., up to the date of the court's decision minus any amount he or she earned from other sources up to the date of the decision.

Whether backpay is decided by the jury or the court depends on the type of discrimination alleged and statute giving rise to the claim.

- Backpay decided by jury

  - Age (ADEA)

  - Intentional race discrimination (Section 1981)

  - Intentional discrimination by public employer (Section 1983)

- Backpay decided by judge

  - Sex, national origin, religion (Title VII)

  - Disability (ADA)

  - Disparate impact discrimination (Title VII)

Compensatory damages

Compensatory damages compensate the employee monetarily for emotional distress or any other type of injury that may result from the alleged intentional discriminatory conduct.

Compensatory damages, where available, are decided by the jury.

Punitive/liquidated damages

Punitive damages punish the employer for malicious conduct, and deter other employers from engaging in similar conduct in the future.

In 1999 the Supreme Court held in <u>Kolstad v. American Dental Association</u>, that a jury may award punitive damages under Title VII or the ADA in any case where the employee proves that the employer engaged in intentional discrimination, regardless of the severity of the misconduct. The Court also recognized, however, that an award of punitive damages against an employer is not appropriate when the employer is held liable for the discriminatory conduct of one of its employees, but can prove that it acted in good faith to comply with Title VII or the ADA by undertaking affirmative efforts to prevent discrimination, such as implementing a formal anti-discrimination policy.

Punitive damages, where available, are decided by the jury. Government entities cannot be held liable for punitive damages.

Frontpay

Frontpay is an award that compensates for lost future earnings.

Frontpay is decided by the judge in most jurisdictions. The law on this issue, however, is unsettled.

Reinstatement

Ordering that the employee be rehired into the position he or she held prior to the discriminatory action.

Reinstatement is decided by the judge.

Attorneys' fees

Payment of a reasonable fee to the employee's attorney along with reimbursement for litigation related expenses.

Key point
The availability of attorneys' fees makes employment discrimination claims different from most types of litigation. A prevailing employee's attorney

may recover a reasonable fee from the employer (calculated based on the number of hours spent on the case times a reasonable hourly rate), regardless of whether the attorney actually charges the employee for her services. This means that the more time an attorney puts into a case, the more difficult it will be to settle it for a reasonable amount of money.

Damage caps

The Civil Rights Act of 1991 imposes the following caps on the combined amount of punitive and compensatory damages that may be recovered by an employee in cases alleging intentional discrimination based on race, gender, national origin, religion, or disability.

14-100 employees	$50,000
101-200 employees	$100,000
201-500 employees	$200,000
500+ employees	$300,000

There is no statutory cap on backpay, frontpay, or attorneys' fees. A court may award backpay, front pay, and attorneys' fees in any amount proved at trial, in addition to compensatory/punitive damages.

The damage caps established by the Civil Rights Act of 1991 apply only to claims of discrimination under Title VII of the Civil Rights Act (sex, race, national origin, religion) and the Americans with Disabilities Act (disability). In some cases employees may have additional federal remedies that are not subject to damage caps. For instance, 42 U.S.C. § 1981, which prohibits intentional race discrimination in the making and enforcement of contracts (including all employment relationships), contains no monetary cap on available compensatory damages (See Chapter 6, **Race discrimination**).

Compensatory and punitive damages are not available in age discrimination cases under the ADEA; however, the jury may award liquidated damages equal to twice the amount of lost wages.

Appeals

After the jury returns the verdict, the losing side may ask the court to reverse the verdict or grant a new trial. This is an extremely difficult task because it usually means convincing the court that it made serious procedural errors during the trial or that the case should have never even gone to trial. Judges are human and do not easily admit mistakes; therefore, the chances of getting relief from the trial court are slim. However, in order to challenge the jury's verdict before the court of appeals, the losing party must first give the trial judge the opportunity to correct any mistakes.

The federal Court of Appeals consists of a three judge panel that bases its decision solely on the written and oral arguments of the attorneys for both sides, and the written record of testimony and evidence introduced at trial. The appellate court, like the trial court, will defer to the jury's decision and will not set it aside even if they would have decided the case differently than the jury. The appellate court also defers to the expertise of the trial judge in deciding what evidence should be admitted at trial. However, the appellate court will closely scrutinize whether the trial court properly instructed the jury as to the applicable law and ruled properly in deciding whether the employee presented sufficient evidence to warrant submitting the case to the jury in the first instance.

Chapter 5

Resolving employee disputes/charges

The high cost of litigation, the inability of administrative agencies and the courts to keep up with the constant flood of employment claims, and dissatisfaction with the jury system has caused many employers to consider alternative methods of resolving employment disputes.

Indeed, the vast majority of discrimination claims are settled prior to trial. Settlements may be negotiated face-to-face between the parties, or their attorneys, or by the use of mediation. In mediation, a neutral third party attempts to help the parties reach a mutually agreeable settlement. Almost every case will involve some type of mediation, whether it is conducted by the EEOC investigator, a judge, or an independent third party selected by the parties precisely for the purpose of mediating a dispute.

In addition to settling disputes after they arise, some employers have successfully avoided the court system altogether through the use of mandatory arbitration.

Alternative dispute resolution (ADR)

Many employers already practice basic ADR without knowing it. The simple principle underlying ADR is that disputes are best settled quickly before they fester and grow. A model ADR program strives to bring disputes to the attention of key decision makers as soon as they arise.

Open door policies

One way to resolve disputes quickly is to encourage employees to bring grievances to their immediate supervisors. An open door policy requires a commitment by managers to listen and react to employees. Managers must be trained to listen for particular problems which may need special investigation. For example, allegations of sexual harassment or safety concerns should be referred to senior management for full investigation and resolution. The failure to promptly and appropriately react to such allegations may later create liability for the employer.

Successful open door policies permit employees to take their grievances to different levels in the organization. Often, the immediate supervisor is the cause of the problem or lacks authority to resolve the grievance. In such a case, the employee should be permitted to discuss the problem with higher managers.

Open door policies may prevent litigation to the extent they correct problems before employees become upset enough to seek a lawyer or before an individual is injured. Also, records from a good faith open door policy may evidence an employer's efforts to accommodate an employee. Ultimately, a disgruntled employee may still pursue litigation even after exhausting options under an open door policy. Employers should be cautious in dealing with chronic troublemakers who may use meetings under the open door policy as fodder for a court complaint.

Internal mediation

A more formal way to resolve complaints is to designate an individual to whom employees can take complaints. Sometimes called an ombudsman, the mediator functions as a go between, trying to work out the underlying dispute. The intervention of a mediator may be more successful than an open door policy when a personality conflict is involved or where the employee is embarrassed to make the complaint. A good mediator can help both sides see issues objectively and assist them in reaching a mutually satisfactory solution.

Whether internal mediation succeeds depends on the skill and credibility of the mediator. Employees must trust the individual to keep their confidences. Employees must also perceive that the mediator has enough clout with management to effect change. It is important for key decision makers to publicly support the mediation process so supervisors down the line will give the mediator the respect necessary to succeed.

From a management standpoint, mediation conserves managerial resources when compared to an open door policy because only one individual is primarily focused on the dispute. Also, it is generally easier to find one person with good listening and problem-solving skills than to teach all managers those skills. A mediator is more likely to investigate complaints promptly and thoroughly because the mediator should have fewer operational responsibilities than line supervisors.

At worst, if mediation fails, the employer has had an opportunity to flesh out the employee's complaint and assess the merit of its own position. If the employee chooses to go to court, the employer will already have much of the information necessary to defend the suit.

EEOC mediation program

The EEOC actively encourages the voluntary resolution of discrimination charges through mediation. Since 1997 each EEOC district office has implemented a formal mediation program. The district office will review each filed charge to determine whether it may be appropriate for mediation. If so, the charging party is contacted to see if he or she is willing to participate in the mediation process. If the charging party agrees to attempt to resolve the charge through mediation, the employer is contacted. If both parties agree to mediate the dispute, the charge enters the mediation process.

Mediations are conducted by mediators employed by the EEOC or provided by outside contractors such as the Federal Mediation and Conciliation Service (FMCS). Many district offices also rely on pro bono (unpaid volunteer) mediators. All mediators receive training in mediation techniques and federal anti-discrimination laws, however, the degree of expertise and knowledge can vary. Because effective mediation requires that the mediators be neutral and the mediation remain confidential, each field office has established mechanisms to separate the mediation process from the EEOC investigation process.

An employer should seriously consider participating in the mediation process. Mediation provides the opportunity to resolve the charge at an early stage, before either party has invested substantial time and effort. Although an effective mediator will push both parties to compromise their respective positions in order to reach a settlement, the parties are under no obligation to do so. Even if the charge does not settle, during mediation the employer may learn information about the nature of the employee's charge that will assist it in defending the charge.

Mandatory arbitration

Some courts recognize that an employer and employee at the outset of the employment relationship may agree to submit any future employment disputes to arbitration. Under mandatory arbitration, both the employer and employee agree to submit any employment related dispute to a neutral arbitrator and agree to be bound by the arbitrator's decision. Unlike mediation, in which the parties are free to reject any resolution that is proposed by the mediator, once the parties agree to submit their dispute to arbitration, they are bound by the arbitrator's ultimate decision. From an employer's perspective there are both significant benefits and drawbacks to such an arrangement.

Benefits of mandatory arbitration

- Significant cost savings are derived from quicker, simpler proceedings with limitations on prehearing discovery.

- Litigation, including appeals, can last 3 to 8 years before a final decision is rendered. Studies show that on average arbitration resolves disputes in 8 to 9 months.

- An arbitrator's decision and award is final and binding and may be appealed only under limited circumstances.

- Arbitrators, unlike juries, are usually experienced professionals who understand the applicable law and have resolved similar disputes in the past.

- Arbitrators have proven track records and reputations that can be quickly researched before being selected, while juries are unpredictable.

- Arbitration results are usually private and confidential, thereby avoiding negative press and publicity.

Drawbacks of mandatory arbitration

- Employees are more likely to use the arbitration process to challenge decisions because of its reduced costs and increased efficiency.

- Judicial review of arbitration decisions is very limited. If an arbitrator makes a mistake of law, it is not grounds for reversal. However, if a judge commits the same error, the mistake may be corrected on appeal.

- Employees may feel their individual rights are being eroded by the arbitration system.

- Whether the law allows mandatory arbitration is unsettled in many jurisdictions. Thus, litigation may arise over the very issue of whether a claim should be decided by a court or an arbitrator, creating the type of cost and delay that arbitration was designed to avoid in the first place.

EEOC's policy statement on mandatory arbitration

The EEOC holds the position that mandatory arbitration agreements are contrary to federal civil rights laws. In July 1997, the EEOC issued a "Policy Statement on Mandatory Binding Arbitration of Employment Discrimination Disputes as a Condition of Employment," in which it reaffirmed its long-standing opposition to mandatory arbitration. In its statement, the EEOC admonished courts for releasing claims to mandatory arbitration and reminded the courts that mandatory arbitration agreements substitute private dispute resolution systems for the public justice system Congress intended to enforce employment discrimination laws. In the EEOC's view, arbitration has inherent limitations, such as the inability to afford employees a trial by jury. The EEOC's disapproval of arbitration rests strongly on the presumption that the employee is a weaker party, coerced into arbitrating prospective claims, agreeing only out of a lack of understanding of the process or fear that they will be fired or not hired if they refuse to sign. The EEOC stated that it will investigate and process discrimination complaints even where the employee has agreed to arbitrate employment disputes, especially where the agreement was secured under coercive circumstances (for example, as a condition of employment).

Given these contrasting benefits and views, mandatory arbitration is not for every employer. Any employer considering mandatory arbitration should consult with an attorney to determine whether such a policy will be enforceable and whether it makes sense given the employer's particular circumstances.

Resolving employee disputes/charges

Chapter 6

Race discrimination

Discrimination on the basis of "race" or "color" generally refers to discrimination on the basis of an immutable characteristic or trait that is associated with race, including skin color, facial features or perceptions and stereotypes about members of certain races. Federal law prohibits employers from discriminating against employees and applicants based upon race.

Race discrimination prohibited under Title VII

Title VII of the Civil Rights Act of 1964 prohibits public and private employers of 15 or more employees from discriminating against any person with respect to the terms, conditions or privileges of employment because of the individual's race or color. Title VII's prohibition against race discrimination extends to all aspects of an employment relationship, including hiring, promotion, evaluation, training, job assignment, compensation, discipline and termination.

An individual who believes that he or she has been discriminated against on the basis of race, however, may not proceed directly to federal court and file suit under Title VII. Rather, he or she must first file a charge of discrimination with the EEOC or comparable state agency (see Chapter 4, **Anatomy of a discrimination charge and lawsuit**). After the agency concludes its processing of the charge and gives notice to the individual of his or her right to sue, he or she may file a complaint in federal court within a specified period of time.

Potential liability

If the individual prevails on a Title VII race discrimination claim in court, the potential damages are substantial. A successful plaintiff may recover reinstatement or front pay, backpay, and reasonable attorneys' fees and costs. In cases of intentional discrimination, a plaintiff also may recover compensatory and punitive damages. The total amount of compensatory and punitive damages that a plaintiff may recover is capped at an amount ranging from $50,000 to $300,000 depending upon the size of the employer. These damage caps are not, however, absolute. If a plaintiff also alleges a race discrimination claim under Section 1981 of the Civil

Rights Act of 1866 (as described below), the Civil Rights Act of 1991 specifically states that the damage caps are not applicable.

Who is protected

Under Title VII, individuals of all races and color are protected against discrimination. Courts also have recognized that individuals of a particular race or color are protected against discrimination by persons of the same race under Title VII. In addition, individuals who file race discrimination claims against their current or former employers are protected against retaliation from those employers.

Types of claims

Disparate treatment claims

Under Title VII, a plaintiff who alleges race discrimination may pursue a claim under the theory of "disparate treatment." An employer engages in unlawful disparate treatment when it intentionally discriminates against an individual or treats the individual less favorably than other similarly situated individuals because of his or her race. Courts also have found disparate treatment under Title VII when an employer discriminates against an individual because he or she is in an inter-racial marriage or has a close relationship with someone in a protected group.

Defense tips

An employer can defend against a disparate treatment claim by demonstrating that its treatment of an individual was based on a legitimate business reason that had nothing whatsoever to do with the person's race. In addition, the employer can bolster its legitimate business reason defense by establishing that the individual complaining of race-based discrimination was, in fact, treated in the same manner as other, non-protected employees under similar circumstances.

After the employer offers such evidence, the employee then must prove that the employer's legitimate business reason either is "false" or was not the true motivating reason behind the employment decision. If the employee cannot do this the employer must prevail.

Disparate impact claims

A plaintiff alleging race discrimination under Title VII also may bring a claim under a "disparate impact" theory. A disparate impact claim typically targets an employer's policy or practice that appears to be non-discriminatory, but that adversely affects individuals or a particular race or color more than others. To prove disparate impact, the employee must demonstrate that a significant disparity exists between the racial composition of the individuals holding the jobs at issue and the racial composition of the qualified individuals for these jobs in the relevant labor market. If the employee establishes a disparate impact, the employer must then prove that the employment policy or practice is job-related and consistent with business necessity. An employee is not required to prove that the employer intentionally discriminated against a protected group of individuals to recover under the disparate impact theory.

For example, a manufacturing company had a policy that required applicants for certain unskilled positions to have a high-school education or an equivalent standardized certificate. An African American applicant challenged the policy under the disparate impact theory by proving that it had a disproportionately negative effect on African American candidates. The employee demonstrated that a substantial disparity existed between the number of African American employees in the manufacturing positions at issue and the number of qualified African American applicants for the positions. In light of the fact that the employee proved the policy had a disparate impact, the employer was required to demonstrate that a high school education or its equivalent was necessary to the successful performance of the unskilled manufacturing positions. The employer argued that the policy was designed to improve the overall quality of the workforce. The court found the employer's reason for the policy did not constitute business necessity.

Another illustrative disparate impact case was based on a city's policy that required all firefighters to be clean-shaven. An African American employee challenged the city's policy by arguing the policy had an adverse effect on African American men who disproportionately suffer from pseudofolliculitis barbae, which causes their faces to become infected after shaving. The city successfully defended the policy by proving that firefighters are required to wear respirators which do not fit properly unless the person is clean shaven. On the other hand, employees have successfully challenged no-beard grooming policies where respirator use was not at issue.

Defense tips

An employer who is confronted with a disparate impact claim can defend itself by demonstrating that the challenged employment practice or test does not, in fact, have a disproportionately adverse impact on individuals of a certain race or color.

For example, an employer might show that Caucasian applicants pass or fail a certain pre-employment aptitude test at approximately the same rate as Asian applicants. Such a showing would refute the claim that the test had an adverse impact on Asian applicants. Additionally, because most plaintiffs use expert statistical evidence to demonstrate a disparate impact, the employer can attack the credibility of the statistical evidence either directly through its own expert witness or indirectly by offering evidence to challenge the factual foundation or methodology behind the plaintiff's statistical evidence. Finally, if a plaintiff establishes that a particular employment practice does have an adverse impact on members of a certain racial group, the employer may still prevail by showing that the practice is job-related and consistent with business necessity.

Racial harassment claims

Title VII also prohibits employers from engaging in racially motivated harassment or from tolerating a work environment which is offensive or hostile to individuals of a particular race or color. To prove racial harassment, the employee must establish the same elements of a hostile environment claim that are required in sexual harassment cases. (See Chapter XX, **Sexual harassment**.)

The employee must also prove that the employer is liable for the racial harassment. In cases where a supervisor is not involved, an employee proves racial harassment by showing that:

- he was subjected to repeated and pervasive harassment based upon his race

    and

- the employer knew or should have known of the harassment

    and

- the employer failed to take prompt and appropriate action to prevent or remedy the situation.

In cases involving racial harassment of an employee by a supervisor, courts have been applying the standards recently established by the U.S. Supreme Court in the context of sexual harassment. Employers are presumptively liable for racial harassment by supervisors that occurs in the course and scope of their employment. However, employers may avoid liability if they prove that:

- the employer had a policy against racial harassment which included a complaint procedure

    and

- the employee acted unreasonably in failing to make a complaint under the policy.

Defense tips

An employer may defend against a racial harassment claim by demonstrating that the complaining employee was not subjected to repeated or pervasive harassment based upon his race. Casual remarks or isolated comments or jokes with racial overtones are insufficient to show "harassment" under Title VII. An employer also may defeat a non-supervisor racial harassment claim by showing that prompt and appropriate remedial action was taken as soon as the offensive comments or conduct were known. If the claim involves harassment of an employee by a supervisor, the employer can defend itself by proving that they had a policy against racial harassment and the employee unreasonably failed to make a complaint under the policy.

Retaliation claims

Title VII protects individuals against retaliation by their former, as well as current, employers. Recently, the U.S. Supreme Court concluded that employers cannot provide negative references about a former employee to a prospective employer simply because the individual has filed a race discrimination claim against them.

Defense tips

When asked by a prospective employer about an individual's work performance, an employer should provide factual information only and avoid any appearance of retaliation. A cautious employer may choose to provide only the dates of employment, position held and rate of pay.

Intentional race discrimination prohibited under Section 1981

Section 1981 of the Civil Rights Act of 1866 (Section 1981) prohibits public and private employers, with the exception of the federal government, from intentionally discriminating against an applicant or employee on the basis of race or color. Unlike Title VII, coverage under Section 1981 does not require any minimum number of employees. The Civil Rights Act of 1991 established that Section 1981 applies to all aspects of employment relationships, including the "making, performance, modification and termination of contracts, and the enjoyment of all benefits, privileges, terms and conditions of the contractual relationship."

Unlike Title VII, Section 1981 does not require an individual to file a charge with any federal or state agency. Therefore, an individual who claims race discrimination under Section 1981 may proceed directly to federal court and file suit under Section 1981.

Potential liability

An individual who succeeds in proving a Section 1981 claim in court may recover reinstatement or front pay, back pay, attorneys' fees and costs, and punitive and compensatory damages. Under Section 1981, there are no statutory limits on the potential punitive and compensatory damage awards which a successful plaintiff may recover.

Who is protected

Under Section 1981 individuals of all races are protected against discrimination, including Caucasians. Section 1981 also has been applied to cases in which a Caucasian employee is discriminated against for marrying or associating with non-Caucasian persons.

Intentional discrimination prohibited

A plaintiff who sues under Section 1981 must establish that his or her employer intentionally discriminated against him or her on the basis of race. Thus, Section 1981 claims are comparable to disparate treatment claims under Title VII. In fact, the standards of proof and liability applied to Section 1981 claims are identical to the standards which are applied to Title VII disparate treatment claims. Claims alleging disparate impact, however, cannot be brought under Section 1981.

Defense tips

An employer must defend against a Section 1981 claim in the same manner as a Title VII disparate treatment claim. The employer must demonstrate that the employment decision at issue was based upon a legitimate business reason or that it treated the plaintiff in the same manner as another individual of a different race under similar circumstances.

Federal contractors and subcontractors

Executive Order 11246 prohibits federal contractors from discriminating against any employee or applicant on the basis of race, color, religion, sex or national origin. It also requires federal contractors to take affirmative action to ensure that all applicants and employees are employed without regard to race or color. Executive Order 11246 is enforced by the Office of Federal Contract Compliance Programs (OFCCP). If a contractor fails to satisfy the obligations imposed by Executive Order 11246, it may be barred from obtaining federal contracts in the future. See Chapter 18, **Affirmative action**.

Practical pointers

An employer **MUST**:

- Make all employment decisions without regard to race or color.

- Have a policy prohibiting racial harassment and outlining a specific complaint procedure.

- Communicate its policy against racial harassment to all employees.

- Consistently enforce all policies, including those prohibiting racial harassment.

- Conduct a prompt, thorough investigation of any racial harassment complaint and take disciplinary action against the alleged harasser if warranted.

- Monitor its policies and practices to ensure that they do not result in a disparate impact on a protected group.

- Train supervisors regarding non-retaliation principles.

Practical pointers

An employer **MAY**:

- Decline to hire a minority applicant as long as the decision is based on a legitimate reason such as the individual's lack of relevant skills or work history.

- Impose discipline for poor performance or absenteeism on a minority employee as long as the same standards are applied to all employees under similar circumstances, regardless of race or color.

- Promote a non-minority employee over a minority employee if that employee is better qualified to perform the duties of the new position and the decision is not based on race or color.

- Prohibit all employees from telling racial jokes, using racially derogatory terms or displaying racially insensitive materials in the workplace.

- Maintain neutral policies and procedures that are job-related and consistent with business necessity.

Practical pointers

An employer **MAY NOT**:

- Require applicants to own a car to be hired if driving their own car is not part of the job duties of the position for which they are applying, as this may result in a disparate impact claim.

- Discipline or terminate an employee for complaining about alleged race discrimination by co-workers or supervisors.

- Assign employees to shifts or departments based on race.

- Refuse to promote an employee because that employee is married to someone of a different race.

- Use a pre-employment aptitude test which excludes minority applicants much more frequently than non-minority applicants unless the test is related to the duties of the position being applied for and is consistent with a business necessity.

- Provide a negative employment reference for a former employee because he or she filed a charge of race discrimination against the company with the EEOC.

Chapter 7
National origin discrimination

Discrimination on the basis of "national origin" refers to discrimination based on differences in ancestry, heritage or national background. All employees possess a particular ancestry, heritage or national origin, therefore, all employees have protected status.

National origin discrimination prohibited under Title VII

Title VII of the Civil Rights Act of 1964 (Title VII) prohibits employers with 15 or more employees from discriminating against any person with respect to the terms, conditions or privileges of employment because of the individual's national origin. Discrimination on the basis of national origin in hiring, promotion, training, job assignment, discipline or termination is prohibited. Title VII also prohibits employers from discriminating against former employees in retaliation for claiming national origin discrimination.

An individual seeking to bring a national origin discrimination claim under Title VII must first file a charge of discrimination with the EEOC or the appropriate state fair employment practices agency. Only after receiving a notice of right to sue from the EEOC may an individual file suit in court. Chapter 4, **Anatomy of a discrimination charge and lawsuit** contains an overview of EEOC and court procedures.

Potential liability

Damages available under Title VII for intentional national origin discrimination include reinstatement or front pay, back pay, and compensatory and punitive damages within the statutory caps. Under the damage caps, larger employers face greater liability for compensatory and punitive damages than smaller employers.

Who is protected

The EEOC maintains that Title VII extends protection against national origin discrimination beyond national ancestry to characteristics generally identified with individuals from particular ancestral backgrounds. This extended protection includes the following:

- marriage or association with a person of specific national origin

- membership in, or association with, an organization identified with or seeking to promote the interests of a certain national origin

- attendance at, or participation in, schools, churches, temples, or the like that are generally used by persons of a particular national origin

- use of an individual's or spouse's name that is associated with a particular national origin

- membership in a particular Native American tribe.

National origin discrimination under Section 1981

Section 1981 of the Civil Rights Act of 1866 (Section 1981) prohibits discrimination based on national origin in the making and enforcing of contracts. Section 1981 applies to the making, performance, modification and termination of a contract as well as the "enjoyment of all benefits, privileges, terms, and conditions of the contractual relationship." Under Section 1981, employment is a contractual relationship, even if there is no written contract. Unlike Title VII, which applies only to employers of 15 or more persons, Section 1981 contains no minimum number of employees. Individuals seeking to bring claims under Section 1981 may go directly to court without first having to file a claim with any federal or state agency.

Potential liability

Damages available under Section 1981 for cases alleging national origin discrimination include reinstatement or front pay, back pay, and unlimited compensatory and punitive damages.

Who is protected

Section 1981 protects persons who are subjected to intentional discrimination solely because of their ancestry or ethnic characteristics.

Citizenship and national origin discrimination under the Immigration Reform and Control Act

The Immigration Reform and Control Act (IRCA) prohibits discrimination in hiring, recruitment, referral for a fee or discharge on the basis of national origin or citizenship. Charges of unfair immigration-related employment practices proscribed by IRCA may be filed with the Office of the Special Counsel. However, if an individual has filed a charge with the EEOC alleging a violation of Title VII, he or she may not file a charge based on the same set of acts with the Office of the Special Counsel, unless the charge is dismissed by the EEOC because it is beyond the scope of Title VII.

Potential liability

IRCA's discrimination provisions only apply to employers with 4 or more employees. IRCA's discrimination provisions only apply to employer's with 4 or more employees. An employer who violates IRCA's discrimination provisions may be ordered to pay a civil penalty, backpay and reasonable attorneys' fees.

Who is protected

IRCA prohibits employers from discriminating against any individual on the basis of national origin and prohibits employers from discriminating against "protected individuals" based on citizenship status. Under IRCA, protected individuals include:

- United States citizens or nationals

- permanent resident aliens

- temporary resident aliens

- refugees and individuals granted asylum.

Challenged employment practices

English-only rules

A policy that requires employees to speak English **at all times** in the workplace is assumed to be unlawful unless the employer has a strong business justification for such a rule. The EEOC contends that English-only rules at work are "a burdensome term and condition of employment" and it presumes such rules violate Title VII. However, if the rule is applied only to job-related conversation and speech, it may be permissible if the employer sufficiently notifies its employees of the rule.

Title VII does not protect an employee's ability to express his or her cultural heritage in the workplace. Moreover, conversing with other employees during work hours is a privilege of employment, and employers can impose boundaries on this privilege. Therefore, when a bilingual employee can readily comply with the rule and noncompliance is a matter of individual preference, English-only rules during work hours may not violate Title VII. A foreign accent that does not interfere with the employee's job duties is not a legitimate justification for an adverse employment decision.

Examples
One court held that the termination of an employee for casual use of a Spanish phrase in violation of a work rule was illegal under Title VII. The work rule was informally conveyed and not sufficiently publicized. Moreover, the application of the rule to the employee's use of the phrase while performing a routine duty was not justified.

Conversely, a city lawfully refused to hire a Filipino applicant as a clerk on the grounds that his accent made him difficult to understand. The court held that the decision not to hire was justified because oral communication with the public was a primary function of the job, thereby creating a reasonable business necessity.

Citizenship requirements

Discrimination on the basis of citizenship is a violation of IRCA. In addition, Title VII prohibits an employer from using a citizenship requirement as a pretext for national origin discrimination. For an individual to prove that a citizenship requirement is a pretext for national origin discrimination, he or she would have to show, by use of statistical or other evidence, that an adverse employment decision based on alien status resulted in discrimination on the basis of national origin.

Height and weight requirements

Height and weight requirements may have the effect of discriminating against persons of particular national origins. An employer may impose height or weight requirements only if the requirements are necessary to perform the job.

Example
A city's requirement that all applicants for fire fighter positions meet a height requirement discriminated against Hispanics. The city failed to show the requirement was job-related.

Practical pointers

An employer **SHOULD**:

- Fully inform employees of the necessity for any English-only workplace rules. If an employer believes it has a business necessity for requiring its employees to speak only English at certain times, the employer should inform its employees of the circumstances when speaking only English is required and the consequences for violating the rule.

- Take immediate and appropriate corrective action when alerted to the possibility of a claim of national origin discrimination. An employer is responsible for acts of harassment committed by co-workers on the basis of national origin where the employer knew or should have known of the conduct, unless it can demonstrate it took immediate and appropriate corrective action.

- Use caution when making any employment decision based on a worker's accent or manner of speaking. The EEOC has determined that denying an employment opportunity because of a worker's accent or manner of speaking will be considered discrimination based on national origin unless the employer can establish a legitimate, nondiscriminatory reason for its action.

- Apply all work rules uniformly. Rules that favor individuals of one national origin over another may violate Title VII.

Practical pointers

An employer **MAY NOT**:

- Make an employment decision based on an individual's marriage to someone of a different national origin.

- Establish height or weight requirements that are not related to the position governed by the requirements. A city's requirement that all applicants for fire fighter positions meet a height requirement was held to discriminate against Hispanics. The employer failed to show the requirement was job related.

- Permit a work atmosphere where derogatory remarks or jokes are allowed. Depending on the frequency and seriousness of the comments and on the employer's knowledge, courts have found violations of Title VII where derogatory remarks are uttered by co-workers. For example, one court found that a manager's reference to an employee as a "dumb Mexican" shortly after rejecting another Mexican-American trainee for an insurance agent's job was enough evidence of discrimination to bring the trainee's case to trial.

- Assign an individual of a particular national origin to a certain community of workers because of his or her national origin. It may violate Title VII to assign Hispanics to Hispanic communities because of their national origin.

- Establish requirements that either exclude foreign-trained individuals or require applicants be foreign-trained. This requirement may violate IRCA and would violate Title VII if the requirement had an adverse impact on a particular national origin but was not job-related. Professional certification requirements are considered job-related.

Chapter 8

Religious discrimination

Title VII of the Civil Rights Act prohibits employment discrimination based on an individual's religious observances, beliefs or practices. Title VII also protects an individual who does not have any religious beliefs. Therefore, it is illegal for an employer to discharge, discipline, promote, transfer, hire or not hire an individual on the basis of her religion or lack of religious beliefs. It is also illegal for employers to discriminate against former employees in retaliation for claiming religious discrimination. In addition, an employer may have to take affirmative steps to reasonably accommodate the religious practices of its employees. Title VII applies to all employers, both public and private, with 15 or more employees.

Religious corporations, associations, educational institutions and societies may use religion as an employment qualification without violating Title VII's prohibition against religious discrimination. For example, a Catholic college may require an instructor of Catholic religious history to be a Catholic.

Definition of "religion" as protected by Title VII

Whether an employee's or applicant's beliefs are protected by law depends upon whether those beliefs meet the definition of "religion." The EEOC defines religious beliefs as "moral or ethical beliefs as to what is right and wrong, which are sincerely held with the strength of traditional religious views." This includes "all aspects of religious observance and practice, as well as belief." Legally protected religious beliefs are not limited to organized or traditional religions but also include individual religious beliefs. Religious beliefs which are only a matter of convenience will not be protected.

Examples of religions protected by Title VII include:

- Catholicism

- Protestantism

- Buddhism

- Judaism

- Seventh Day Adventists

- Black Muslims

- Jehovah's Witnesses

- Sikhs

- Native American Church

- Church of God

- Christian Scientist

Notice of religious beliefs and practices

Employees may have special needs based upon their religious beliefs, such as time off work to observe religious holidays. Employers are not required to accommodate religious beliefs (for example, grant time off work) until the employee informs the employer that she requires accommodation for her religion. Employers also may require employees to identify the religious belief that conflicts with their ability to perform their job. For instance, an employee must be able to articulate the religious belief which requires her to take time off work. Employees must cooperate with an employer's reasonable attempt to accommodate their religious beliefs and may not insist on a particular form of accommodation.

Accommodation of religious practices

Employers must accommodate reasonable practices based on their employees' religious beliefs unless to do so would create an undue hardship on the employer's business. As a general rule, an employer must make reasonable attempts to accommodate its employees' religious needs, based on the employer's size, operating costs, cost of making the required accommodation and any other relevant factors. Reasonable practices include allowing employees to wear non-controversial insignia and clothing, or permitting days off to observe religious holidays. Unreasonable practices include inflammatory insignia or clothing that creates a safety hazard.

As an example, in one court case employees claimed religious discrimination because they were prohibited from broadcasting a religious radio station over their employer's public address system. The court rejected the employees' claim, finding that the employer had reasonably accommodated the employees' religious practices by allowing them to listen to music on headsets or on individual radios at their workstations.

An employer does not have to accommodate an employee's religious beliefs if the employer is able to establish that accommodation would create an undue hardship on the employer's business. The employer must show an actual imposition on coworkers or disruption of the work routine to establish an undue hardship. Whether an undue hardship exists is determined on a case-by-case basis, considering the particular facts of each case.

Below are the most common requests for religious accommodation made by employees.

Work schedules

The most frequently requested religious accommodation is for time off work for observance of religious holidays or the Sabbath. These requests fall into two categories:

1. additional days off to observe specific religious holidays

   and

2. schedule and/or shift adjustments to accommodate religious practices or beliefs.

Where possible, employers must accommodate requests under these two categories. For example, employers may grant additional time off for religious observances in the following ways:

- allowing employees to use personal days or vacation time.

- permitting additional days off without pay if the employee does not have any paid days off available.

- arranging a voluntary substitution or swap with another employee.

- permitting the employee to make up the lost time on a different day (such as a weekend)

- permitting flexible arrival and departure times to make up for lost time.

With regard to an employee's request for certain days/times/shifts based on his religious beliefs, an employer may have a bulletin board available for employees to post their requested shift change to seek volunteers willing to swap or adopt flexible work schedules for individuals in need of a religious accommodation. Employers do not have to accept the accommodation proposed by the employee, so long as the accommodation offered by the employer is reasonable. For instance, a Catholic police officer who objected to guard duty at an abortion clinic was not automatically entitled to exemption from this duty. Instead, the city's offer to transfer the officer to another police district that had no abortion clinics was a reasonable accommodation.

In a unionized work place, accommodation of one employee's religious beliefs may create a conflict with the provisions of a collective bargaining agreement. For example, an employee may request not to work on Saturdays based on his religious beliefs, but lack the seniority under a collective bargaining agreement to have Saturdays off. Typically, in such instances, it is considered to be an undue hardship to require other employees to violate the terms of a collective bargaining agreement to accommodate an employee's religious request. Generally, an employer is not obligated to deny another employee his job or shift preference established under the seniority system of a collective bargaining agreement in order to accommodate an employee's religious needs.

Dress codes

As a general rule, dress and grooming codes are permissible under Title VII as long as they, like other work rules, are enforced evenhandedly. More specifically, dress and grooming policies may be applied to employees whose job responsibilities require extensive contact with the public, or to employees whose jobs would be made hazardous by particular forms of dress. One court held that an employer's enforcement of a dress code which required employees to wear a bow-tie when working as garage cashiers was not religious discrimination. In that case, an employee who was a Jehovah's Witness claimed that she was singled out for enforcement of the dress code policy. However, she failed to produce any evidence that non-Jehovah's Witness employees were permitted to violate the policy. The employer also submitted records showing that other employees were disciplined for violating the dress code policy. For these reasons, the employee's religious discrimination claim failed.

Even with a valid uniform policy, situations may arise in which an employee's religion requires him to wear specific clothing or a specific mode of dress that is inconsistent with the employer's policy. In such instances, employers who strictly apply their uniform policies without considering whether they can accommodate the employee's religion may be discriminating against the employee. Instead, the employer should determine:

- whether the employee has a bona fide religious belief which conflicts with the uniform policy

- whether the employee has informed the employer of this fact

- whether the employer can reasonably accommodate the employee without suffering undue hardship.

For example, a car rental agency which requires attendants to wear a uniform, including a baseball hat, may have to accommodate a Muslim employee's request to wear a traditional head covering instead of a hat.

Grooming standards

A number of religions and religious sects forbid followers from cutting or shaving their hair and/or facial hair. To the extent that an employee or applicant believes in and follows these religious tenets, his or her sincerely held religious beliefs could conflict with an employer's grooming standards. Under these circumstances, Title VII requires the employer to reasonably accommodate the employee's religious beliefs unless such accommodation will result in undue hardship for the employer. For example, an airline that requires ticket agents to be clean-shaven must allow an accommodation to an employee whose religious faith requires him to wear a beard.

Commonly asked questions and answers

Q. **May an employer require employees to attend a meeting where a short religious ceremony is conducted?**

A. No. Requiring employees to attend a religious ceremony violates Title VII.

Q. **Must an employer hire an additional employee to accommodate an employee who cannot work on his Sabbath?**

A. No. Spending more than a insignificant amount, such as hiring a new employee, would be considered an undue hardship on an employer.

Q. **Does an employer have to accept an employee's preferred accommodation?**

A. No. So long as an employer offers some form of reasonable accommodation, it does not have to be the employee's first preference. For example, suppose an employee requests a day off work to observe a religious holiday and proposes to make the time up by working two extra hours the other work days. The employer may allow the employee's request, may require the employee to make up the time on Saturday, or may require the employee to use a vacation day. Any of these alternatives would be a reasonable accommodation.

Q. **What are an employer's obligations if it requires employees who use respirators at work to be clean shaven and an employee refuses to shave based on religious beliefs?**

A. Legitimate safety rules ordinarily are considered superior to religious practices or standards. Observance of such rules may often be made absolute conditions of employment. The employer should determine whether it can accommodate the employee's religious beliefs. Examples of accommodation include transferring the employee to a position that does not require respirator use, or, if respirator use is only a minimal part of the job, having other employees take over the functions that require respirator use. If there is no reasonable accommodation available and if the requirement that the employee be clean shaven is legitimate, the employer should be able to terminate the employee on the grounds that retaining the employee is an undue hardship.

Q. Does an employer have to accommodate an employee's religious beliefs that could result in the employer's violation of federal or state law?

A. No. For example, an employer is not required to accommodate an employee's sincerely held beliefs preventing the employee from obtaining a social security card, where under federal law, an American citizen is required to obtain a social security number.

Practical pointers

An employer **MAY**:

- Grant an employee time off to observe religious holidays not observed by co-workers who ascribe to different religions.

- Permit employees to swap shifts to accommodate an employee's religious needs.

- Discipline an employee for taking an **unapproved** leave to attend a religious ceremony.

- Instruct employees not to preach religion to co-workers or customers.

- Display nativity scenes and other religious symbols, provided the employer is a private, non-government entity.

- Require employees to adhere to job-related or safety-required dress and grooming standards.

- Refuse to hire an additional employee in order to accommodate another employee who requests time off to observe her Sabbath.

- Discipline an employee for telling co-workers that their lives are offensive to God.

- Offer to transfer an employee to another shift or position as a reasonable accommodation of her religious beliefs.

- Offer floating holidays, flexible arrival and departure times or use of employee lunch hours to make up for lost time to accommodate the employee's religious beliefs.

- Require employees to articulate the particular religious belief which mandates time off work.

- Refuse to hire an employee whose requested religious accommodation **requires** the employer to violate other federal laws.

Practical pointers

An employer **MAY NOT**:

- Discipline an employee for requesting a vacation day to observe a religious holiday.

- Require employees to attend weekly prayer session held during working hours.

- Refuse to hire an applicant because she is a devout follower of a particular religion (exceptions exist for religious organization employers).

- Violate one employee's bona fide seniority rights under a collective bargaining agreement to accommodate another employee's religious needs.

- Require employees to donate time and/or money to a religious charity.

- Require an employee to demonstrate that she is devout in the observance of all aspects of her religion in order to observe specific religious holidays.

Chapter 9

Sex discrimination

Title VII of the Civil Rights Act of 1964, the Equal Pay Act, and the Pregnancy Discrimination Act collectively protect employees and applicants for employment from gender discrimination, typically known as sex discrimination. Gender discrimination includes sexual harassment, pregnancy discrimination, pay discrimination because of gender, as well as discrimination because of gender in any term or condition of employment.

Impermissible discrimination may also occur when neutral policies have a disparate impact on a particular gender. For example, employment decisions based on an employee's height, weight, or appearance may favor one gender more than the other and therefore be unlawful. In limited circumstances, discrimination based on sex may be allowed if gender constitutes a "bona fide occupational qualification" for the position in question (for example, it is permissible to refuse to hire a male for the position of a womens' washroom attendant).

Statutes prohibiting gender discrimination apply to both genders. Although most cases involve females, males also are protected from sex discrimination and sexual harassment under Title VII and from pay discrimination under the Equal Pay Act.

Pay discrimination

Title VII of the Civil Rights Act prohibits gender discrimination in all terms and conditions of employment, including compensation or pay. Pay discrimination based on gender also is prohibited by the Equal Pay Act. The Equal Pay Act is part of the Fair Labor Standards Act. The Equal Pay Act prohibits discrimination in pay for work that requires equal skill, effort and responsibility and which is performed under substantially similar working conditions, when pay differences are based on gender. The Act, unlike Title VII, is limited to gender-based differentials in compensation and does not prohibit discrimination in other aspects of employment, such as hiring, promotion, and firing. For example:

- A female who applies for and is denied a job as an engineer in favor of a less qualified male applicant may have a claim under Title VII, but would not be protected by the Equal Pay Act.

- A female engineer who is paid less than a male engineer for work requiring equal skill, effort and responsibility may have a claim under Title VII and the Equal Pay Act.

Employers covered

The Equal Pay Act covers all employers who employ 2 or more employees.

When is an employer liable for pay discrimination

An employer violates the Equal Pay Act by providing less compensation to one employee than to another employee of the opposite gender when the two employees are performing jobs that have the same purpose, require equal skill, effort and responsibility and which are performed under similar working conditions at the same establishment. In determining equal skill, effort and responsibility, the substance of the work performed must be examined, not simply the job title or classification given by the employer. With respect to "similar working conditions," one must consider the employee's surroundings, the hazards encountered by the employee, and the work schedule. For example:

- A hospital violated the Equal Pay Act when it paid male janitors more than female housekeepers for similar general cleaning responsibilities.

- A bank did not violate the Equal Pay Act when it paid female employees more than male employees pursuant to its formal written seniority and merit systems.

- An insurance company lawfully paid a higher salary to a male underwriter with eight years of experience than to a female underwriter with six years of experience.

As long as an employer applies rules, wage standards and job classifications equally to employees of both genders, any resulting pay differential will not violate the Equal Pay Act. Difference in compensation is allowed if the difference is due to:

- a seniority system

- a merit system which is organized, structured and systematically administered

- a system which measures earnings by quality or quantity of production

- a differential based on any factor other than gender (for example, shift differential).

Unlike under Title VII of the Civil Rights Act, an employee need not prove intentional discrimination to prevail on a claim under the Equal Pay Act.

Potential liability

An employee may bring a private cause of action under the Equal Pay Act to recover any impermissible pay differential for the period within 2 years of bringing his or her claim (3 years in case of willful violations). Additionally, under the Equal Pay Act, an employee may recover an equal amount in liquidated damages (an amount set by judgment or an ascertainable amount of damages – here the amount lost by the employee as a result of the employer's violation), as well as attorneys' fees and costs. Under Title VII, an employee may also recover the pay differential, including attorneys' fees and costs. However, unlike the Equal Pay Act, an employee must file a charge of discrimination with an administrative agency prior to bringing a claim under Title VII.

Pregnancy discrimination

The Pregnancy Discrimination Act of 1978 (PDA) provides that an employer may not refuse to hire, terminate or otherwise discriminate against an employee because of her pregnancy, childbirth, decision to abort or other pregnancy related medical conditions. A number of states have approved measures protecting a woman's right to breast feed.

An employer should be mindful of the following issues to avoid potential liability under the PDA:

- Disabilities associated with pregnancy and childbirth must be covered under health insurance plans to the same extent as other kinds of temporary disabilities.

- Reinstatement and accumulation of seniority must be protected to the same extent as for other types of disabilities.

- An employee seeking extended leave after childbirth for child care reasons is not considered disabled unless there are complications due to the childbirth. If, however, the employer generally grants leave of absence for personal non-disability reasons, new mothers should be provided extended leave beyond FMLA leave.

- Conversely, if extended child care leaves are offered to female employees who are physically able to work, male employees must receive the same benefit.

Under the PDA, pregnant employees must be treated the same as other employees for all employment related purposes. Therefore, employers are not required to afford special treatment to pregnant employees. For example, an employer need not permit excessive absences where such absences are related to pregnancy, as long as comparable absences of non-pregnant employees are not permitted.

In addition to the PDA, other federal laws also protect pregnant employees and new parents from discrimination in the workplace, including the Family and Medical Leave Act of 1993 (FMLA) (see Chapter 13, **Family and Medical Leave Act**) and the Americans with Disabilities Act of 1990 (ADA) (see Chapter 12, **Disability discriminatio**n).

For example, the FMLA requires employers with 50 or more employees to provide up to 12 weeks of unpaid leave of absence to care for a newborn, newly adopted or foster child. If a husband and wife work for the same employer, they may be limited to a combined total of 12 weeks of leave in a 12 month period to care for a newborn, newly adopted or foster child. Many states provide similar protection. Additionally, the United States Supreme Court has held that reproduction is a major life activity protected under the ADA. Thus, employment policies that adversely affect employees with reproductive disorders or associated conditions may violate the ADA.

Fetal protection

Title VII of the Civil Rights Act of 1964 prohibits an employer from imposing a fetal protection policy that discriminates on the basis of gender without regard to an employee's ability to perform her job. A safety-based fetal protection policy may, however, successfully be defended as a bona fide occupational qualification (BFOQ) if the policy is limited to instances in which pregnancy actually interferes with an employee's ability to perform her job.

The Supreme Court held unlawful an employer's fetal protection policy that excluded fertile female employees from manufacturing jobs that would expose them to conditions that might harm their fertility and/or unborn children. Finding that the relevant consideration was the employees' ability to perform their jobs, the Court rejected the employer's attempted defense which was based on its desire to avoid harm to unborn children and its concern for future liability to children who were injured in the womb as a result of their mother's exposure to fetal toxins.

The issue of fetal protection was debated between OSHA, which required that employers protect employees from exposure to fetal toxins, and the EEOC, which insisted that the employee's right to work in jobs of his/her choosing outweighed concerns for the safety of unborn children. In a leading case, the Supreme Court came down squarely on the side of the EEOC. The Court brushed aside the employer's concern for future liability to unborn children and stated that as long as the employer has made the dangers clear, it should not be held liable in the future for negligence.

Employers who use fetal toxins in the workplace should:

1. Determine whether there is any practical means of using an alternative non-toxic substance or eliminating employee exposure to the toxin.

2. Determine whether the substance affects both genders, in which case a non-gender-based protection policy can be adopted.

3. Thoroughly inform employees of the dangers of exposure to the toxin so that they may make informed judgments as to whether to accept jobs in the affected areas. Employee education may include oral discussions, written notice or educational films. This warning must be sufficiently clear to cause a jury to reject the employee's future claim that he/she did not really understand the danger. All warning materials should be carefully preserved for use in future litigation.

4. Require employees who wish to work in the affected area sign a waiver stating that they have been apprised of the danger and that they knowingly and voluntarily agree to work in the affected area.

Employees who choose to expose themselves to fetal toxins cannot waive the rights of their unborn children. Potential liability for employers is catastrophic since such children need not sue until they reach adulthood – eighteen years after the alleged injury has occurred. Employers must hope that the Supreme Court's optimistic view that employers will not be held liable to employees' children if the employer has not been negligent will be borne out in future litigation or that Congress will amend Title VII to eliminate this no-win situation for employers.

Commonly asked questions and answers

Q. May an employer implement job classification or longevity requirements for pay increases and promotions or cap the maximum amount of a pay increase?

A. Yes. These requirements and other similar rules are permissible as long as they apply equally to both genders, even if the requirement results in differences in compensation between employees of the opposite gender.

Q. Does an employer violate the Equal Pay Act or Title VII if it raises the salary of a female employee to correct a wage disparity?

A. No. An employer may correct a gender-based wage disparity by increasing the pay of the lower paid employee. An employer may not lower employees' wages to correct a disparity.

Q. May an employer pay two persons of opposite genders different salaries based on their titles?

A. Only if the employees' titles reflect genuine differences in their job requirements and performance.

Practical pointers

An employer **MAY**:

- Apply a gender-neutral pay differential based on a seniority system, merit system, or any factor other than gender, as long as the policy is applied equally to employees of both genders.

- Correct a gender-based disparity in wages by increasing the pay of the lower paid employee.

- Decline to provide extended maternity leave for child care reasons other than complications from childbirth, if the employer does not provide similar extended leaves for other personal non-disability reasons.

- If using fetal toxins in the workplace, have employees who wish to work in the affected area sign a waiver stating that they have been apprised of the danger and that they knowingly and voluntarily agree to work in the affected area.

Practical pointers

An employer **MAY NOT**:

- Pay two employees of the opposite gender different compensation, if the difference is based on gender.

- Provide less protection of employment rights to pregnant employees than other disabled employees.

- Fail to give extended child care leaves of absence to male employees, if they are offered to female employees.

- Impose a safety-based fetal protection policy against only female employees, if the toxic substance affects both genders.

- Take adverse employment action against a pregnant employee in anticipation that her pregnancy will require special treatment.

Chapter 10

Sexual harassment

Definition of sexual harassment

The Equal Employment Opportunity Commission (EEOC) defines sexual harassment in employment as unwelcome sexual advances, requests for sexual favors and other verbal or physical conduct of a sexual nature. These acts constitute sexual harassment when:

- submission to such conduct is made either explicitly or implicitly a term or condition of an individual's employment

  or

- submission to or rejection of such conduct by an individual is used as the basis for employment decisions affecting the individual

  or

- the conduct has the purpose or effect of unreasonably interfering with an individual's work performance or creating an intimidating, hostile, or offensive working environment.

Examples of harassment include:

- offering an employee a benefit, such as a job, promotion, pay increase, or trip out of town for agreeing to sexual demands

  or conversely,

- punishing an employee for not agreeing to a sexual advance by discharging or refusing to hire the employee, assigning the employee to disagreeable tasks, not promoting the employee or not granting him or her a salary increase.

Hostile environment harassment occurs when an employer creates or permits the existence of an atmosphere of sexually offensive conduct or speech so pervasive and offensive that a reasonable employee could not tolerate working under such conditions. The employee does not have to show that the offensive conduct affected his/her promotion, job, or other employment benefits. A hostile environment might exist where supervisors or employees routinely proposition or fondle employees, tell vulgar jokes, or make demeaning sexual comments Offensive e-mails may also create a hostile environment.

Employees may also claim that harassing conduct constitutes unlawful misconduct under state law, such as intentional infliction of emotional distress.

Potential liability

Potential remedies under Title VII include reinstatement, backpay, attorneys' fees, injunctive orders and compensatory and punitive damages. Because Title VII caps available compensatory and punitive damages at $300,000 or less, depending on the size of the employer, a plaintiff who brings a successful state law claim may obtain a higher recovery.

Who can commit harassment?

Harassment can be committed by both male and female supervisors, co-workers and even non-employees, such as vendors, contractors and customers.

Same sex harassment

In 1998, the Supreme Court ruled that Title VII prohibits sexual harassment by members of the same sex (that is, males sexually harassing males or females sexually harassing females). In Oncale v. Sundowner Offshore Services, the Court allowed a male employee to sue his employer for sexual harassment allegedly committed by his male co-workers. More recently, a female employee who was subjected to name-calling and accused of promiscuity by her female co-workers was permitted to proceed with her hostile environment claim. The relevant issue is whether one individual is harassing another individual because of that person's gender. To further clarify, a male employee who is subjected to sexual harassment by his male supervisor will be able to make a claim under Title VII if he shows that female employees were not similarly harassed. The employee is able to make a claim because he can show that he was harassed because of his male gender. By contrast, a male employee who is harassed by his co-workers because he is gay will not be able to state a claim under Title VII. In this situation, the employee is being harassed because of his sexual orientation, not because of his gender. Harassment based on sexual orientation is not prohibited under Title VII.

When is an employer liable for sexual harassment?

The Supreme Court clarified the standards for employer liability for sexual harassment in 2 major decisions which it issued in 1998. Whether an employer will be held liable for sexual harassment depends, in part, on whether the harasser is a supervisor or a co-worker of the harassed employee.

Liability for sexual harassment by supervisors

- **Automatic liability for adverse employment action**
  Employers are automatically liable if the harassing supervisor takes a tangible employment action, such as a discharge, demotion or undesirable transfer, against the complaining employee.

- **Affirmative defense available if no adverse employment action**
  If the supervisor's harassment does not result in a tangible employment action against the complaining employee, then employers may avoid liability if they prove:

  - they exercised reasonable care to prevent and correct promptly any sexually harassing behavior

    and

  - the employee unreasonably failed to take advantage of any preventive or corrective opportunities provided by the employer or to avoid harm otherwise.

Courts have held that having an anti-harassment policy with complaint procedures is an important consideration in determining whether the employer has satisfied the first step of the affirmative defense. The second step of the defense is often proved by showing that the employee unreasonably failed to make a complaint under the anti-harassment policy.

Liability for sexual harassment by non-supervisors

While the Supreme Court did not address employer liability for sexual harassment by co-workers or non-employees in its landmark 1998 decisions in this area, the lower courts have generally agreed that an employer is responsible for such conduct only if it knew or should have known of the conduct and failed to take appropriate corrective action.

Are supervisors personally liable for sexual harassment?

Most courts have held that supervisors may not be held personally liable under Title VII for sexual harassment. However, supervisors may be named as individual defendants in state law claims brought with the Title VII suit.

How do we know if sexual harassment has occurred

Not all sexual conduct is sexual harassment. In order for conduct to constitute sexual harassment it must be "unwelcome." Consensual flirtation, dirty jokes, or even sexual relations will not be considered harassment unless they are **unwelcome**. However, mere acquiescence or passiveness to sexual advances does not necessarily mean that such conduct is welcome.

In determining whether a sexual advance is welcome, the EEOC and the courts examine the conduct of the complaining party. Provocative dress or conversation by a complaining party, for instance, may be construed to suggest that an advance was welcome. On the other hand, the fact that the victim engaged in some provocative behavior does not necessarily mean that he or she welcomed all sexual advances or conduct. Each claim must be examined to determine whether the particular conduct complained of was unwelcome.

When does unwelcome sexual conduct become harassment

Unwelcome sexual conduct becomes harassment when it creates a working environment which is unreasonably intimidating or offensive. The standard is both objective and subjective. That is, a work environment is not considered hostile unless a reasonable person would find it offensive and the complaining employee actually perceived it as offensive.

To constitute harassment, the conduct must substantially affect the work environment. A hostile environment claim usually requires a pattern of conduct with a repetitive and debilitating effect. Some of the factors to consider in determining whether the work environment is so hostile or offensive as to constitute harassment are:

- whether the conduct is verbal, physical or both

- how frequently the acts are repeated

- whether the conduct is hostile and patently offensive

- whether the conduct is perpetuated by a co-worker or supervisor

- whether other people joined in the activity

- whether the conduct was directed at an individual or a group.

Although hostile environment cases usually involve a pattern of conduct, a single instance of extremely severe sexual conduct, as for example, the touching of intimate body areas, may suffice to create a claim.

Must we adopt a "zero tolerance" policy?

Even though isolated jokes and comments are insufficient to establish a hostile environment claim, many employers have concluded that the only practical way to avoid liability for a hostile environment is to adopt workplace policies banning all sexually oriented jokes, comments and behavior from the workplace. Their reasoning is that it is unworkable to discipline some employees but not others for sexually oriented behavior or to initiate discipline policies for the second or third, but not the first, sexually oriented joke. While "zero tolerance" policies go beyond the requirements articulated by the courts or the EEOC, they have the virtue of being simple to understand and enforce.

Sexual harassment outside of work

Conduct which would otherwise constitute sexual harassment which is performed before or after work or off the employer's premises constitutes sexual harassment if it is job-related.

For example, claims of sexual harassment may arise from conduct at informal after work get-togethers, company parties, and out-of-town business trips.

The employer's obligation to correct problems

An employer is automatically liable if a harassing supervisor actually takes an employment action against the complaining employee. The only way to avoid liability for this type of harassment is to make sure that the problem does not occur. Employers should carefully monitor supervisory actions with respect to discipline, discharge, evaluation, salary increase, promotions and assignments to ensure that the supervisor's actions are unrelated to gender.

In the case of hostile environment harassment or situations where supervisors threaten to, but do not actually, condition employment consequences on an employee's response to unwelcome sexual advances, liability is usually imposed only as a result of an employer's failure to have a policy prohibiting harassment or to adequately follow-up and investigate claims of sexual harassment. Employers have a duty to reasonably respond to, investigate, and resolve claims of sexual harassment. The employer should promptly, adequately and completely respond to a problem or complaint no matter how it learns of the problem, documenting its investigation along the way. The responsive action should be appropriate in light of the evidence uncovered. For example, if the victim quits due to the harassing environment, the employer may be required to offer reinstatement to the victim.

How do we know when we have done enough?

The courts evaluate the employer's response by looking at:

- whether the employer had a policy against sexual harassment

- whether that policy was adequately publicized to employees

- whether the policy had an adequate complaint procedure

- the promptness and adequacy of the employer's responses to employee complaints.

The employer's response must be prompt. Tacit approval of the harassment by delay may be as damaging to the employer as the conduct itself.

The employer may also be held liable for improper or inadequate responses. Employers have been held liable in the following situations:

- when a verbal reprimand proved ineffective and the employer took no further action when informed of the harasser's persistence

- where co-workers harassed the victim for over four years. When informed of the problem by numerous complaints, the supervisor took no action other than occasionally reminding employees of the company policy against the conduct. No investigation or action occurred until the EEOC charge was filed

- where a victim's first level supervisor responsible for correcting the problem was also the harasser.

Prevention

Employers have an affirmative duty to prevent sexual harassment and to make a reasonably diligent inquiry into situations which might constitute sexual harassment. The employer cannot wait for the problem to come to it. Some of the preventive actions the employer should adopt include:

- affirmatively raising the subject with all employees (both to emphasize opposition to such conduct and to make employees aware of the problem)

- expressing strong disapproval of the misconduct

- informing employees of their rights and the consequences of violating the employer's policy against harassment.

The most important action the employer can take to prevent harassment and to minimize liability is to develop and effectively implement an explicit policy against sexual harassment and to communicate this policy clearly and regularly. Furthermore, the most recent decisions by the Supreme Court clearly underscore the importance of having and communicating a policy against harassment and discrimination in order to limit an employer's potential liability for punitive damages.

What to include in a policy

The written policy should include:

1. A prohibition against sexual harassment as defined by the EEOC. In order to be clear, the policy should give illustrations of the prohibited conduct and specify that the policy applies to all employees.

2. A provision stating that sexual harassment will result in discipline up to and including discharge.

3. An assurance that the complaining employee will not be retaliated against for bringing complaints in good faith and that his/her complaint will be kept confidential to the extent consistent with the employer's need to investigate.

4. A complaint procedure by which employee complaints of sexual harassment may be promptly addressed. The procedure should give employees a limited choice of company officials to complain to in order to ensure that the employee is not required to bring his/her complaint to the alleged harasser.

To ensure that all employees know and understand the policy, it should be routinely distributed to all current employees on a periodic basis and to all new employees at the time of hire.

Investigating a claim

Careless investigations may result in claims by the alleged harassers against the employer, including claims for wrongful termination, grievances, or claims for defamation or discrimination. It is thus imperative that the employer fully investigate both sides of the story and not disseminate specific information about the matter except to those with a need to know.

All complaints of sexual harassment must be promptly and thoroughly investigated. It is insufficient to simply elicit a denial by the alleged harasser. The employer should try to obtain all potentially relevant information, including the accounts of witnesses and other parties. Relevant information may include eyewitness accounts, statements from individuals with whom the complainant discussed the incident, statements from co-workers who may have observed the alleged victim's demeanor either before or after the claimed incident and statements from other employees who may have been harassed by the alleged harasser. Both the accused and the accuser should be given the opportunity to offer any evidence or identify any witnesses who can support their version of events.

The employer's primary duty is to investigate claims thoroughly. The investigation should protect the privacy of the accuser, the accused and any witnesses in so far as is consistent with its duty to investigate. In most instances, fairness will require that the accused be apprised of the identity of the person who is accusing him/her of sexual harassment in order that he/she has a genuine opportunity to respond to the claims.

To preserve the confidentiality of the investigation, witnesses should be questioned in private. Witnesses should not be asked leading questions or told the exact allegations, unless disclosure is necessary to obtain information from the witness. The witnesses should be told to keep their conversations with the investigator confidential.

For hostile environment claims, the investigation should determine the nature, frequency, context and intended target of the complained-of conduct. Some of the issues the employer might explore include:

- Did the alleged harasser single out the victim?

- Did the victim participate?

- What was the relationship between the victim and the alleged harasser?

- Were any remarks hostile and derogatory?

Each step of the investigation should be thoroughly documented.

An investigation can result in three conclusions:

1. **Sexual harassment has occurred.**
   This situation is the easiest for the employer to handle. The employer's duty if the allegations prove to be true is to take appropriate corrective action. What that action will be depends on the individual circumstances of each case, including the severity of the misconduct.

   Appropriate corrective action may include:

   - discharge

- reprimand

- suspension or probation of the harasser

- reinstatement with back pay of the victim

- transfer with equal pay and equal duties for the victim

- transfer or demotion of the harasser

- discipline of supervisors or co-workers who failed to report the harassment.

The employer should also make follow-up inquiries. This includes investigating to ensure that there are no other victims and, in the case of a hostile environment, that the hostile environment has been completely cured.

The employer should develop a checklist of remedial actions to ensure that it has taken all necessary steps to deal with the complaint. A sample checklist might include the following:

- Was the complaint investigated promptly and thoroughly?

- Were the offenders appropriately dealt with (reprimand or discharge)?

- Was the victim made whole, including the restoration of benefits and lost opportunities?

- Has any hostile environment been eradicated?

- Have steps been taken to avoid future problems?

2. The allegation was unfounded.
When the employer finds the allegation to be unfounded, it should thoroughly document its investigation, clearly stating its reasons for concluding that the allegation was unfounded. In such cases, it may be in the best interests of both the accused and the accuser to separate them in the workplace if possible.

A potentially difficult issue is what to do about the employee who made the unfounded accusation. Title VII protects employees who have opposed discriminatory employment practices from retaliation even if their claims of discrimination are unfounded. An employee who has made a good faith allegation of sexual harassment cannot be disciplined even if he/she was wrong.

On the other hand, there may be instances where employees knowingly lie to attempt to cause the discharge of a fellow employee with whom they have a dispute or to protect themselves from a negative employment action by a supervisor. Where an employee has knowingly made a false allegation, he/she may be disciplined or even terminated. In order to defend any subsequent charge of retaliation, there must be strong evidence that the employee knowingly misrepresented the facts.

3. **Based on the evidence, the employer cannot make a determination.**
    In these instances, the employer should document its investigation and clearly state why it cannot reach a determination. It should advise the accused individual of the results of its investigation, remind him/her of the employer's policy against harassment and inform him/her that any proven incidents of harassment in the future will subject him/her to discipline. The employer should also advise the accuser of the results of its investigation and encourage him/her to bring forward any further evidence or to apprise it of any future complaints. It may also be appropriate for the employer to separate the accused and the accuser. Such separation may not always be possible, particularly if it would result in a less favorable job for the alleged victim.

Practical pointers

An employer **SHOULD**:

- Maintain a written policy which is communicated to all employees defining and strictly prohibiting sexual harassment and informing employees to whom they bring harassment complaints.

- Ensure that all employers sign a form acknowledging their responsibility to read and learn the terms of the written policy.

- Train employees that sexual harassment is prohibited and will result in discipline.

- Ensure that supervisors are trained to recognize sexually harassing behavior and know to report the conduct and/or discipline the employee(s) who engaged in the behavior.

- Promptly and thoroughly investigate any complaints of sexual harassment and take appropriate remedial action sufficient to stop the harassment if the investigation concludes harassment has occurred.

- Investigate claims of same gender harassment the same as claims of opposite gender harassment.

- Refuse to disclose any specific information about a sexual harassment complaint or the actions it took with respect to the complaint, except to those with a need to know.

- Discipline an employee who has committed sexual harassment before/after work or outside the workplace, if the conduct was job-related.

- Follow up with employees who previously complained of harassment to ensure that the harassment has been stopped.

- Develop institutional "checks" on the authority of lower-level supervisors and managers, such as requiring that at least two management persons be responsible for all significant employment decisions.

Practical pointers

An employer **SHOULD NOT**:

- Put off investigating, or neglect to investigate thoroughly, a complaint of sexual harassment.

- Tolerate inappropriate and unwelcome sexual harassment on the theory that "boys will be boys."

- Repeatedly warn employees to stop engaging in sexual harassment if the warnings do not stop the conduct. Rather, more severe discipline is required.

- Discipline an employee who makes a good faith allegation of sexual harassment, even if the employer's investigation determined no harassment occurred.

- Transfer a victim of sexual harassment to a lesser position to end the harassment.

- Treat harassment claims made by men as a joke or refuse to take them seriously.

- Decide against investigating a harassment claim because the complaining employee asked that the matter be kept confidential.

- Assume it has no responsibility for harassment committed by contract employees or vendors at its worksite.

- Permit lewd conversation and publication of sexually explicit jokes, photos or cartoons.

- Allow employees to forward sexually offensive e-mails around the office.

Chapter 11

Age discrimination

Employers in the private sector are covered by the Age Discrimination in Employment Act (ADEA) if they employ 20 or more employees for each working day in each of 20 or more calendar weeks in the current or preceding year. In 2000, the U.S. Supreme Court ruled that state governmental entities are not subject to the ADEA. Therefore, state employees cannot sue their employer under the ADEA. However, it remains unsettled whether local government entities, such as municipalities, are immune from suits brought under the ADEA. Additionally, public sector employees are still subject to state laws that prohibit age discrimination.

The ADEA protects any employee over the age of 40 from employment discrimination based upon age. The law does not contain an upper age limit. All intentional discrimination is prohibited. This includes considering age in discipline, setting wages, promotions, assigning shifts, etc. Employers may also be prohibited from creating a hostile working environment based on age. This includes age-based comments, threats and age-related teasing. If an employee proves an ADEA violation, he or she may be hired, reinstated, promoted or given backpay, including lost wages and other benefits, depending on the circumstances. If the evidence supports a finding that the employer's actions were willful, then the employee may also be awarded damages equal to two times the loss of wages and benefits.

Proving age discrimination claims

Age discrimination charges must be filed with the EEOC within 180 days of the discriminatory act. In states that have similar laws and administrative agencies that also accept age discrimination claims, a charge may be filed with the EEOC as late as 300 days after the alleged violation. The typical elements of proving age discrimination involve showing that:

- the employee was 40 years old or older at the time of the alleged discrimination

  and

- the employee was performing according to the employer's legitimate expectations

  and

- others who are younger than the employee were treated more favorably. The younger employee need not be under age 40 if the age gap is significant (usually 10 years difference in age is considered significant).

The presence of these factors will be enough for an employee to prove age discrimination if an employer fails to articulate a legitimate, non-discriminatory reason for its action.

Specific issues related to downsizing

With any downsizing or reduction in force, issues under the ADEA may arise (see the companion **Survival Guide** for a discussion of WARN). In downsizing cases, an employer who releases an employee protected by the ADEA while simultaneously treating younger employees more favorably must provide a legitimate reason for its decision. In addressing downsizing issues, employers should prepare for the legal concerns but should realize that there are also non-legal considerations. The downsizing may affect the morale of employees remaining after the layoff who will closely scrutinize the fairness of the process used to determine who is laid off.

In addressing the legal and non-legal considerations, employers should:

1. **Develop a standard**

   - How have prior layoffs, if any, been handled?

   - What role should seniority play in the process?

   - Will employees be allowed to transfer to other positions, including to those that are lower paying, if their jobs are eliminated?

   - Will early retirement incentive programs (ERIPs) play a role?

2. **Prepare and anticipate the reduction in force**

   - Have steps been taken to avoid the reduction?

   - Has the employer instituted a hiring freeze which tends to reassure employees of the employer's fairness?

   - If a hiring freeze across-the-board is not possible, has there been a freeze on those positions identical to or similar to existing positions in which employees are subject to layoff?

   - Has the employer considered a voluntary resignation program?

   - Who will head the management teams to carry out the reduction in force?

- Who will have the final authority regarding reduction decisions?

- Who will serve to review any reduction decisions?

3. Conduct an analysis of the workforce

- The employer should complete a statistical analysis of the workforce in preparation for the reduction in force.

- Statistical analysis should compare the workforce by age, gender and race.

4. Prepare for initial communication to employees

- Has the workforce been advised of the employer's financial position?

- How will the employer communicate the workforce reduction to employees?

- Will communication be made to employees prior to the implementation of the reduction?

- Consider the pros and cons of giving prior notice and of advising employees of the company's intention to reduce its personnel. (Note: notices under the Worker Adjustment Retraining and Notification Act (WARN) may be required.)

5. Develop tests to determine who should be laid off

- Objective tests may include:

  - solely seniority-based

    or

  - straight job elimination.

  Note
  Seniority-based tests should clearly define the type of seniority used (for example, job, company or departmental seniority) and employers should use one definition consistently.

- Subjective judgments of performance are not per se illegal, but because courts and/or juries will closely scrutinize such tests to ensure that discrimination was not part of the subjective analysis employers should:

  - ensure a degree of formality is part of the selection process. This is the most important consideration because an informal, unwritten guideline will provide little protection if an ADEA claim is made

- provide specific guidance to evaluators on work-related criteria. This is one of the most commonly cited deficiencies in ADEA cases

- instruct evaluators to be truthful in their evaluations

- avoid the use of non-performance-based criteria

- try to use more than one evaluator for each employee; each evaluator should make an independent judgment

- consider the possibility that an evaluator may also be laid off subsequently.

- Do not rely solely upon prior performance appraisals. The focus, clarity and forthrightness of prior appraisals may not meet the standards set for evaluating employees in the downsizing. Also, if the scope of a job has changed, the prior evaluation may not reflect how a particular employee will perform in the new job. Finally, prior appraisals are not as valuable because they are completed in the abstract without a need to compare similarly-situated employees.

- If ERIPs are used to reduce the workforce, do not offer more favorable packages to younger employees eligible for the program.

6. Develop safeguards for the entire process

- Determine whether employees should have a chance to comment regarding the evaluations which may lead to layoffs.

- Ensure that all decisions are reviewed by higher levels of management and, just as importantly, by someone in management who has knowledge of the law in this area.

- Determine if there are any adverse effects on protected groups.

7. Communicate the termination decisions

- Great care should be taken in carrying out the layoff and in communicating the decision to those affected by the layoff. Harsh methods can:

  - encourage claims

  - create other causes of action

  - affect the jury's decision.

- Be honest and straightforward regarding the reasons a particular employee was selected to be laid off.

- Consider a procedure for the resolution of disputes.

- Consider out-placement services.

- Exercise caution in hiring for a period of time following the reduction in force.

Older Workers Benefit Protection Act of 1990 (OWBPA)

As part of a downsizing plan, an employer may wish to offer workers protected by the ADEA a separation agreement in exchange for a waiver and release of all rights and claims under the ADEA. The Older Workers Benefit Protection Act of 1990 (OWBPA) establishes the requirements that must be satisfied when an employee waives or releases rights under the ADEA.

Individual waivers under the OWBPA

An individual's waiver of an age discrimination claim will be valid only if:

- it is in writing

- it is written in language understandable to lay persons

- it specifically refers to rights or claims under the ADEA

- the waiver is exchanged for something of value, such as a lump sum payment, **in addition to** that to which the employee is already entitled

- the employee is advised in writing to consult with an attorney prior to executing the release

- there is no waiver of any claim which may arise after the waiver is executed

- the employee is allowed at least 21 days to consider the waiver agreement

- the employee is allowed 7 days after signing to revoke the waiver agreement.

Group waivers under the OWBPA

If a waiver is offered in connection with an exit incentive or other termination plan offered to a group or class of employees, the following requirements also must be met:

- All individuals in the group are given at least 45 days to consider the waiver/release agreement.

- All individuals in the group must be informed of the class, unit or group of employees covered by the program, any eligibility factors for the offer, and the time limits applicable.

- All individuals in the group must be informed of the job titles and ages of all persons eligible or selected for the program and the ages of all individuals in the same job classification or organizational unit who are not eligible or selected.

Pros and cons
of a separation agreement
Pros

- An employer can avoid the cost of litigation (in other words, the amount of time spent by managers during litigation and attorneys' fees) if it is in compliance with the factors listed above.

- An employer can avoid the negative publicity resulting from litigation.

Cons

- If an employer fails to comply with the factors listed above, the separation agreement will not be enforceable and the employer will have given the employee additional money for nothing in return.

- The separation agreement may notify the employee of rights and remedies about which the employee was not aware.

- An employer may set a precedent with other employees who learn that the terminated employee received additional payment in exchange for the release.

Practical pointers

An employer **SHOULD NOT**:

- Tell employees they were fired because of their age or because they could not keep up with the pace.

- Tell employees they will be terminated for refusing to accept severance or early retirement packages in exchange for a waiver of claims, including age claims.

- Tell age-related jokes or make age-related remarks like "you look good for your age," "a fossil like you gets around pretty good" or "I'm surprised you are handling this at your age."

- Make public statements emphasizing youth, freshness, vigor, energy, young blood, younger image or a youth movement.

- Make age-related comments on any evaluation forms or any internal memoranda of any type.

- Make premature statements about downsizing or outsourcing.

- Mention age during the interview process.

Practical pointers

An employer **SHOULD**:

- In a reduction of force, use a selection committee or decision-makers who are older than the affected employee.

- Use a decision-maker who has hired or promoted other older employees or given favorable evaluations to other older employees.

- Have the person who hired or promoted the employee included in the pending employment decision.

- Send a written memo instructing managers that age should not be part of the criteria for any decision.

- Instruct managers to be truthful when evaluating, disciplining and terminating employees.

- Counsel employees for poor performance.

- Use objective, legitimate, non-discriminatory reasons that can be supported with evidence in making employment decisions.

- Instruct all employees involved in the interview process to avoid any references to the applicant's age.

Chapter 12

Disability discrimination

The Americans with Disabilities Act (ADA), the Rehabilitation Act of 1973 and the laws of most states prohibit discrimination against qualified individuals with disabilities. These disability discrimination laws are intended to eliminate situations in which an individual who is qualified to perform the essential functions of a position would be denied an opportunity to fill the position or is treated adversely simply because the individual has a disability which either:

- does not actually prevent successful performance of the essential functions of the position

  or

- can be reasonably accommodated without undue hardship to enable the individual to perform the position

  or

- never actually existed or no longer exists, but is nonetheless believed (wrongly) to exist.

These laws attempt to achieve their objectives through:

- prohibiting discrimination based on an actual or believed disability (as defined) which does not prevent successful performance of a position

- requiring "reasonable" accommodation as necessary to enable a person with a disability to perform the essential functions of the position

- limiting the circumstances under which an employer may make inquiries about an individual's physical or mental health or condition

- prohibiting discrimination based on a non-disabled individual's relationship to or with a person who has a disability

- providing procedures to determine the nature and extent of a disability to resolve questions about the need for accommodation or the nature of required accommodations

- prohibiting discrimination because of an individual's exercise of rights provided by the laws, including the right to complain about treatment that may be inconsistent with the law

- allowing for potentially extensive civil liability for violations of these requirements.

Covered employers

The ADA covers all public employers and private employers with 15 or more employees. A private employer is covered if it employs 15 or more individuals on each working day in each of 20 or more calendar weeks in the current or preceding calendar year. The ADA also covers labor organizations, employment agencies and joint labor-management committees regardless of the number of employees. The Rehabilitation Act covers all government contractors and employees of the federal government, regardless of workforce size.

Disability defined

An individual is disabled under the ADA if he or she:

- has a physical or mental impairment that substantially limits one or more major life activities

- has a record of such impairment

- is regarded as having such an impairment.

In addition, an individual who has a relationship or association with someone who has a known disability is protected by the ADA.

An impairment that substantially limits one or more major life activities

1. **Impairment**
   An impairment is an abnormal physical or mental condition such as blindness, deafness, schizophrenia, bipolar disorder, missing limb(s), disfigurement, chronic debilitating illness (cancer, heart weakness, AIDS, diabetes, migraine in severe cases or arthritis).

The term includes acquired conditions such as:

- substance addiction

- eating disorders

- the long-term or permanent effects of accidents and illnesses.

The term does not include:

- illegal drug use

- criminal behavior

- gender identity conflicts

- compulsive gambling

- temporary impairments regardless of severity (for example, a broken leg that mends without complications or short-term depression at the end of a romantic relationship are not disabilities)

- impairments that are fully corrected with medication or other mitigating measures (for example, the Supreme Court recently held that two nearsighted pilots were not disabled because their eyesight was fully correctable with the use of eyeglasses. Also, the Court recently held that a truck driver whose high blood pressure was controlled by medication was not disabled within the ADA's definition).

The term also does not include conditions that fall within normal ranges of differences between individuals in the general population, including normal range differences in:

- height

- weight

- age-related intelligence

- physical fitness differences that are not results of actual impairments

- athletic ability

- hair and eye color

- tastes and habits

- financial condition

- creativity

- self-discipline

- cosmetic disfigurement such as missing teeth

- temperament

- aggressiveness

- work ethic

2. Substantially limits

An object of the ADA is to assist persons whose impairments create barriers to ordinary life activities not normally encountered by members of the general population. The ADA does not apply to impairments that are relatively insignificant or are common to a majority of persons at one time or another (for example, a severe cold or broken leg).

Generally, whether an individual is "substantially limited" is a case by case determination. However, the Supreme Court has held that an HIV infected individual is "disabled" under the ADA from the moment of infection. The Court concluded that the individual is "disabled" even when the disease is asymptomatic because from the moment of infection the disease alters the individual's cells and chromosomes. Additionally, the infection progresses on a predictable, unalterable course and substantially limits the major life activity of reproduction.

3. Major life activities

Major life activities include:

- caring for one's self

- performing manual tasks

- walking

- sitting

- standing

- seeing

- hearing

- breathing

- speaking

- sleeping

- reproducing

- working

The **Guidance on the ADA and Psychiatric Disabilities** issued by the EEOC states that major life activities may also include:

- learning

- thinking

- concentrating

- interacting with others

Except for the major life activity of working, the other major life activities are considered self-defined. The questions that arise are questions of degree of impairment. However, the major life activity of working is defined by 2 factors:

1. the jobs for which the individual can qualify as a result of the individual's training, abilities and experience

   and

2. the general availability of such jobs within the geographical area reasonably accessible to the individual.

Example
An individual who due to an impairment is unable to perform one particular job, but can perform many other common jobs, may not be considered substantially limited in the performance of working. For example, an individual who is restricted from being a commercial pilot because of poor peripheral vision may not be disabled if the impairment does not impede performance of most other jobs.

In determining whether an individual is disabled under the ADA, the Supreme Court held that courts should consider the remedial effects of medications, prosthetic limbs or other medical aides. If an individual is not substantially limited in a major life activity when medication or mitigating measures are used, the individual is not disabled under the meaning of the ADA.

Record of impairment

Employers are prohibited from discriminating on the basis of a prior record or history of disability. This provision is intended to discourage continued bias based on fears that the disability will reoccur and biases based on unfair stigmatization of individuals. For example, persons with records of heart disease and cancers in remission are protected by this provision.

Regarded as having an impairment

The definition of disability applies to persons who are treated by their employers as though they have an impairment that substantially limits a major life activity, even if the person has no such disability. This provision may become important in 3 ways:

1. an impairment exists but it does not substantially limit a major life activity

2. an impairment exists but it substantially limits a major life activity only because of the attitudes of others

3. no impairment exists.

The important factor to consider is whether the **employer perceived the individual as disabled**. It is irrelevant whether the individual wrongly believed he or she suffered from a protected disability.

For example, an employer who wrongly believes that an employee suffers from HIV, and discriminates based on this belief, will be liable under the ADA even though the employee in fact is in perfect health.

Relationship with a disabled person

The ADA also prohibits discrimination based on the relationship an individual may have with a person with a disability. This provision applies where an employer declines to hire an individual because the individual is related to or works with disabled individuals, because the employer fears it may be responsible for medical care costs through the dependency provisions of its insurance plan, fears that the individual may miss work frequently, or fears that the individual may become infected with a serious disease.

Specific conditions under the ADA

Drug and alcohol use

Illegal use of drugs, whether controlled substances or prescription drugs, is not protected by the ADA regardless of whether employees are addicts or occasional users. Persons who are addicted to illegal drugs are protected if they are not current users. Whether or not an individual is a **current** user depends on:

- the length of time since the last use

- the measures that the individual has taken to prevent future use

- the extent to which the individual appears sincere in attempting to stop use, as opposed to doing what is necessary to gain a reprieve from his employer.

Employers need not accommodate or tolerate:

- former illegal drug users who have not become addicted to the illegal substances

- in-plant or in-office drug traffickers

- employees who currently engage in the illegal use of drugs or are under the influence of drugs at work

Current alcohol use, in contrast, may be protected by the ADA as alcohol addiction. Nevertheless, employers may require that employees not be under the influence of alcohol while at work and may discipline employees for poor work performance caused by alcohol use. Absent a competent diagnosis of alcoholism, the disability laws do not prevent discipline based on use of alcohol, particularly when the alcohol use occurs during work hours or causes an impairment of work performance. A person's status as a drug addict or alcoholic should not be presumed merely from the fact that the person has used drugs or become intoxicated.

Obesity

Weight within normal ranges is not a disability. Where morbid obesity results from physiological or psychological impairment, however, it may be symptomatic of a disability.

Pregnancy

Pregnancy itself is not a disability. Impairments that affect the ability of a woman to conceive or give birth may be a disability, however. The Supreme Court has stated that the ability to reproduce is a major life activity.

Mental disorders

Anxiety, stress, depression, and other mental disorders are recognized impairments under the ADA **if the condition is substantially limiting**. In order to determine whether an impairment is substantially limiting the courts consider:

- the nature and severity of the impairment

- the duration of the impairment

- the expected long-term impact.

As an example, severe depression diagnosed by a health care professional that substantially limits an employee's ability to regularly report to work or significantly restricts the time, manner and duration of work is a protected condition under the ADA.

Under these factors, conditions that are severe, non-temporary, and expected to create a long-term impact are protected under the ADA. Conditions that would not be a disability under the ADA include temporary, non-chronic depression and stress or anxiety such as that experienced due to problems with a spouse or child.

Carpal tunnel syndrome

Whether carpal tunnel syndrome is a disability will depend on the severity, expected duration and extent of any permanent restrictions as compared with the individual's training, experience and abilities for job opportunities. Carpal tunnel syndrome and all other musculo-skeletal conditions such as low back disorders, elbow joint pain and shoulder and finger pain require a competent diagnosis to be regarded as impairments subject to the disability laws.

When is an applicant or employee qualified?

To be protected from discrimination under the ADA, an applicant or employee with a disability must be qualified to perform the essential functions or duties of the position, with or without reasonable accommodation. This requirement has 2 elements.

1. The individual must meet the actual, legitimate requirements of the position, including education, experience, licensing and proficiency. The employer is not

required to relax such requirements in order to permit an individual with a disability to hold the job. For example, if a secretarial position requires that a candidate be able to word process at a rate of 70 words per minute, an applicant with a disability who, even with reasonable accommodation, can attain a speed of only 65 words per minute is not entitled to the position, regardless of disability.

2. Only the ability to perform the essential job functions may be considered. If an applicant cannot drive because of a disability but the ability to drive is not essential to the position, the individual cannot be disqualified. Employers must be careful to ensure that qualifications are essential. For example, an applicant for a sales cashier position cannot be denied the position because his/her disability prevents him/her from standing for long periods of time. In this case, standing is not an essential function because the employee can perform the requirements of the position by using a stool.

Essential functions of the job

A qualified disabled job applicant who can perform the essential functions of a job, with or without a reasonable accommodation, may not be denied the job based upon his or her disability. An applicant's inability to perform marginal job functions cannot be used to disqualify the applicant.

In determining what functions are essential, an employer should consider whether current employees in the job perform those functions and whether the job would be fundamentally transformed if employees did not perform those functions. A function is essential if:

- the job exists to accomplish the function

- only a limited number of employees can perform the function

- the function is highly specialized and an employee is hired for his or her expertise in the area.

Other factors to consider in determining whether a function is essential are:

- the amount of time an employee spends performing the function

- the consequences if the employee were not required to perform the function

- the terms of applicable collective bargaining agreements, if any

- the work experience of previous employees who held the job

- the work experience of employees in similar jobs.

Prior to advertising or posting a job opening, an employer should determine the essential functions of the job. The ADA does not require an employer to develop written job descriptions. However, if an employer has written job descriptions, they should be prepared before the job opening is advertised or posted. Moreover, the job descriptions should focus on the results or outcome of the essential functions of the job rather than the usual methods of achieving those results, and should be updated regularly.

Note

Apart from physical and intellectual essential functions, the ability to attend work on a regular basis, to adhere to safety rules and other reasonable regulations pertaining to the job, the ability to refrain from violence or excessive irascibility, and the ability to work in cooperation with other workers may be considered essential functions.

Employment actions affected by the ADA

Interviews and applications

The ADA protects job applicants from disability-related questions that could be used to screen out qualified individuals with disabilities and ensures that the application process is accessible to persons with disabilities

Accessibility

An employer may not screen out disabled persons from the interview and application process by making those procedures inaccessible. Reasonable accommodations may be required to enable disabled applicants to participate in pre-employment procedures. Reasonable accommodations may include, for example, making the interview room accessible to applicants in wheelchairs or applicants with other mobility restrictions, supplying an interpreter for a hearing-impaired applicant, or providing a reader for a blind applicant.

Prohibited questions

An employer is prohibited from inquiring about a prospective employee's disability on application forms or during interviews. Prohibited questions include those touching upon:

- actual or perceived disabilities

- the nature or severity of the applicant's disability

- past medical history

- workers' compensation history

- hospitalization history

- treatment for drug or alcohol addiction

- treatment for psychiatric problems

- the applicant's need for leave for treatment

- the applicant's physical characteristics, such as missing limbs or scars

- disabilities which may affect the applicant's ability to do the job

- disabilities of the applicant's family members.

Permitted questions

An employer is allowed to determine an applicant's ability to perform a job, including his or her ability to attend work on a regular basis. Permitted questions include:

- whether the applicant is able to perform the essential functions of the job and to demonstrate how he or she would do so

- whether the applicant is able to perform each of a position's listed essential functions

- whether the applicant can meet described attendance requirements

- inquiries into the applicant's previous attendance history, as long as the questions do not refer to disabilities or illnesses.

While an employer is prohibited from refusing to hire an applicant who cannot perform marginal job functions, it is not prohibited from discussing marginal job functions

Selection criteria

Disabled job applicants, like disabled employees, may not be segregated or classified so that their job opportunities are adversely affected. An employer may not use tests or other criteria that tend to screen out the disabled persons.

Tests must be job-related and consistent with business necessity. An employer may not give tests to applicants with impaired sensory, manual or speaking skills in a format requiring the use of those skills, unless the test is intended to measure such skills. Accordingly, a blind applicant may require a reader for a written test or a test in braille. The employer would be required to make an appropriate accommodation, unless sight was necessary to perform the essential functions of the job.

An employer may not refuse to hire an applicant because the applicant is related to or associated with someone who is disabled. This is true even if the employer believes that the applicant would often be absent to care for the disabled person. If the applicant states that she can meet the employer's attendance requirements, then the employer cannot refuse to hire her based on its beliefs to the contrary. An employer is not required to provide reasonable accommodations to those associated with someone who is disabled. The ADA mandates reasonable accommodations only for individuals who are disabled.

Medical examinations

Under the ADA, an employer's ability to require medical examinations depends upon the phase of the employment relationship. An employer may not require a medical examination of an applicant prior to making a job offer.

Once a job offer is extended, the offer may be made conditional upon the results of a medical examination if all employees in same job category have to undergo a medical examination. Information received during medical examinations should be treated as confidential, including keeping the records separate from employees' personnel files.

Some exceptions to the confidentiality requirement exist under the ADA. For example, supervisors may be told of necessary restrictions and/or accommodations. First aid/safety personnel may be told if the disabled individual may need treatment. Additionally, government officials investigating the employer's compliance with the ADA may have access to employees' medical information.

If a medical examination reveals a disability, a job offer cannot be withdrawn unless:

- the reason is job-related and consistent with business necessity and no reasonable accommodation can be made

  or

- the disability would result in a "direct threat," meaning a significant risk of substantial harm to the health and safety of other employees. A recent Ninth Circuit decision has held that a threat to one's own health (the applicant's) does not constitute a direct threat under the ADA.

An employer may not require current employees to undergo a medical examination or ask them if they are disabled, unless the examination is related to the business and consistent with a business need. An employer is not prohibited from conducting voluntary medical examinations as part of an employee health program.

Additionally, if an employee initially provides insufficient information to substantiate that he/she has an ADA disability, an employer **may** require an employee to go to an appropriate health care professional of the employer's choice. If the employer exercises this option, the employer must pay for the examination costs.

Health and safety issues

The ADA does not prohibit an employer from enforcing health and safety standards in the workplace. An employer is not required to hire individuals who are unable to comply with legitimate health and safety standards or who pose direct threats to the health and safety of those in the workplace. To determine whether an individual would pose a direct threat, employers must consider:

- the duration of the risk

- the nature and severity of the risk

- the likelihood that potential harm will occur

  and

- the imminence of the potential harm to others.

Therefore, an employer may not refuse to hire or discharge a disabled employee because of a speculative, or even slightly increased, risk of harm to other employees. An employer's conclusion that a disabled employee would pose a direct threat must be based upon objective, factual information. Moreover, the employer must be sure that a reasonable accommodation would not eliminate or reduce the risk to an acceptable level.

Example
In a recent court case, a firefighter who failed a hearing test did not have an ADA claim because his lack of hearing was a direct threat to the health and safety of others.

Example
A forklift driver who frequently suffered from epileptic seizures could be removed from his position without violating the ADA.

During the employment relationship

An employer may not discriminate against disabled employees in terms of advancement, training, benefits or performance appraisals.

Insurance

An employer may not deny insurance coverage to a disabled employee or subject coverage to different terms and conditions on the basis of the disability. Moreover, an employer may not fire or refuse to hire the disabled applicant because the current health plan does not cover the disability or because the person could increase the employer's heath costs. Additionally, an employer may not take adverse action against an individual who has a family member with a disability.

Fringe benefits

An employer must offer disabled employees the same benefits, including fringe benefits, that it offers other employees. For example, if the employer has a fitness room for employee use, it must be made accessible to disabled employees.

Leave policies

A leave of absence that does not violate an employer's leave policy will almost certainly be considered a reasonable accommodation under the ADA. If an employee requests a leave that extends beyond the policy, the law is less settled. If the requested leave has a definite duration and does not expand the policy too far, it is likely to be considered reasonable. Depending on the particular facts, including the employer's need to fill the position, a longer, more open-ended leave is more likely to be considered unreasonable.

Training programs

Training programs must be accessible to the disabled, as they are to other employees. An employer should not assume that disabled employees are not interested in, or capable of, advancement.

Contractual relations

Employers should ensure that contractors who perform services for the company also comply with the ADA. That is, employers cannot avoid their ADA obligations by contracting out certain responsibilities. For example, an employer may not contract with an organization to provide training at a site inaccessible to disabled employees, unless the organization made the site accessible or changed the site of the training session.

Contrary to the position taken by the EEOC, most courts that have ruled on the issue have held that the ADA does not require an employer to disregard a collectively bargained seniority system in order to accommodate a disabled employee. For example, an employer is not required to allow a disabled employee to displace another employee with greater seniority in order to obtain a position that would accommodate the first employee's disability.

Discipline and discharge

The ADA does not require that quality or quantity performance standards be lowered to accommodate disabled employees. Additionally, disabled employees are subject to the same standards for discipline and discharge. An employer should document performance problems and attempt to remedy them as it would with its non-disabled employees. They should not assume that poor performance is related to the disability. Performance appraisals should be conducted in the same manner for all employees.

Reasonable accommodation

Employer obligations

An employer must provide reasonable accommodation to known physical and mental limitations of qualified applicants and employees with disabilities, unless the accommodation would impose an undue hardship on the employer's business.

The employer must engage in an interactive process with the employee or applicant to determine what accommodation is necessary. An "interactive process" requires that the employer engage in ongoing discussions with the employee and his/her doctor to determine an appropriate accommodation. Recently a federal court held that the interactive process requires larger employers to identify jobs appropriate for reassignment. This duty is imposed on larger employers because in these situations, employees would not be expected to know about available positions.

An employer need not accommodate an applicant who is not otherwise qualified for the position. For example, an applicant who does not meet the educational or skill requirements for the job. Also, the employer is not required to provide the particular accommodation requested by the employee. Any accommodation that will effectively enable the employee to perform the job is sufficient. A reasonable accommodation is a modification to a job, employment practice, or work environment that makes it possible for an applicant or employee with a disability to perform the functions of a job. Examples include:

- making facilities readily accessible to and usable by an individual with a disability

- restructuring a job by reallocating or redistributing marginal job functions

- altering when or how an essential job function is performed

- modifying work schedules

- obtaining or modifying equipment or devices

- modifying examinations, training materials or policies

- providing qualified readers and interpreters

- reassigning an employee to a vacant position for which he or she is qualified

- permitting use of accrued paid leave or unpaid leave for necessary treatment

- providing reserved parking for a person with a mobility impairment

- allowing an employee to provide equipment or devices that an employer is not required to provide.

Courts are unclear as to how much accommodation is "reasonable." Several trends are notable.

- Accommodations that violate the collectively bargained seniority rights of other employees may not be required because such accommodations are generally considered undue hardships.

   Example
   A clerk with little seniority is diagnosed with epilepsy. Irregular sleep patterns aggravate her symptoms, and her physician restricts her to daytime work only. By contract, clerks bid for shifts and shifts are awarded according to seniority. Only the most senior clerks are able to bid successfully for regular daytime shifts. The employer is not required to accommodate the clerk with epilepsy by giving her a daytime shift in violation of the seniority rights of more senior clerks.

- Regular attendance at work is an essential function of every job. Therefore, an employer's reasonable accommodation obligation does not include tolerating excessive absenteeism, even if the absenteeism is due to a disability. Keep in mind, however, that the employee may be eligible for leave under the Family Medical Leave Act, and an employer may not discipline an employee for taking FMLA leave. In addition, granting an employee some time off work may be a reasonable accommodation.

- Extended leaves of absence of indefinite duration are not required.

Example

Assume that an employee suffers an on-the-job injury that crushes his leg and renders him unable to walk. After one year's leave, the employee is still experiencing complications and his physician is unable to predict when or if the employee might be released to return to work. The employer has a policy, which has been applied consistently, that employees who have performed no work for the employer for one year are terminated. In this situation, the ADA does not require the employer to deviate from this policy and grant the employee an indefinite leave of absence.

- An employer is free to establish productivity and attendance standards, so long as the employer's purpose in doing so is not to screen out individuals with disabilities.

Example

If the employer requires all factory employees to produce 1,000 widgets per hour, but a one-armed employee can produce only 750, the employer need not accommodate the one-armed employee by lowering its productivity standard. (However, it may have to provide another accommodation that would allow the employee to produce 1,000 widgets per hour).

- Courts are requiring that determining a reasonable accommodation be an interactive process between the employer and employee. Once an employer is aware of a disabled employee's impairment, it must work with the employee to determine if a reasonable accommodation can be made and to decide on the most appropriate accommodation. Although an employer may have accommodation guidelines in place, each situation should be examined separately.

Example

Even though an employer has a policy stating that employees who have performed no work for one year are terminated, the employer should find out the employee's medical condition prior to terminating the employment at the end of a one year absence. If the employee would be capable of returning to work within 2 weeks, that would be a reasonable accommodation.

Employee obligations

An applicant or employee with a disability who wants to be reasonably accommodated must:

- Make his or her need for an accommodation known to the employer, unless the need is obvious (for example, a mobility-impaired individual's inability to climb a flight of stairs is obvious, as is a hearing-impaired individual's inability to hear a horn honking) or the employer has good reason to know that accommodation may be required. However, an employee is not required specifically to ask for an "accommodation" or to mention a "disability." No specific words need be used in making the request.

- Provide the employer with sufficient information about his or her disability and corresponding limitations to allow the employer to make a reasoned decision about whether an accommodation is necessary and/or helpful. Usually, this means that the employee must submit to a medical examination and must provide a copy of the physician's report regarding his or her limitations to the employer. The examination must not be more extensive than necessary to determine the employee's limitations. For example, an employee who claims to have difficulty walking due to a disability may not be required to submit to an HIV test as part of the examination.

- Cooperate with the employer in determining the type of accommodation that is necessary and/or helpful. This process is interactive and requires both the employer and the employee to "brainstorm." Note that the employee is not necessarily entitled to his or her preferred accommodation. If the employer has another idea that would be effective and easier or less costly for the employer to implement, the employee may be required to accept that accommodation.

Undue hardship

An employer is not required to make an accommodation that would impose an undue hardship on the employer's business or other employees. Undue hardship is an action that presents significant difficulty, disruption, or expense in relation to the size of the employer, its resources, and the nature of its operations, or would require violation of safety/health laws and regulations.

For example, an employer is not obligated to tolerate erratic, unreliable attendance which causes employee shortages and disrupts the operation of business. Whether a disruption occurs, however, depends on the size and resources of the employer.

Light-duty and temporary positions

Many employers use light-duty and other temporary positions to "bridge" employees who are recovering from an occupational injury until they are released to full duty. Typically, these positions require an employee to perform more sedentary or less physically demanding work than he or she ordinarily performs, on a temporary basis.

Employers are not required to **create** new light duty positions as accommodations. However, if light duty positions exist or are created for occupationally injured employees, the employer may be required to offer such a position as a reasonable accommodation.

The employer may designate light duty positions for temporarily disabled employees and limit the length of time an employee may serve in the position. Then, the employee may be removed from the position and placed on disability leave if he/she is unable to return to his/her original position after the designated time. However, if permanently disabled employees are removed from light duty positions, the employer must be prepared to prove that the light duty position was truly a temporary placement.

How the ADA interacts with state laws in defining disability

Employers are required to comply with both the ADA and state and local laws which provide similar or even greater protection to individuals with disabilities. State laws may provide more or less extensive rights than the ADA in a number of respects, one of which is the scope of coverage.

For example, in Texas, current alcoholics and those with AIDS, HIV and other communicable diseases are generally not covered by the state discrimination law. In order for an employer to lawfully exclude an individual with AIDS, HIV or another communicable disease from employment, however, the employer must be able to show that the disease poses a direct threat to the health or safety of others and impairs the individual's ability to perform his or her job.

In California, the disability protections are largely parallel to those provided by the ADA. In one area they are more extensive, however. In addition to prohibiting discrimination based on disability, state law also prohibits discrimination based on medical condition which includes any health impairment related to or associated with a diagnosis of cancer for which a person has been rehabilitated or cured, based on competent medical evidence. Even if such a condition is not a disability or even perceived as such, and accordingly would not be protected under the ADA, it would be protected under California state law.

Because state laws that provide more extensive protections than the ADA remain enforceable, employers are advised to become familiar with the disability discrimination laws in any states where they have operations.

Workplace violence

Employer concerns about workplace violence intersect with employee protections under the ADA when the violence results from a mental impairment. An employer that fails to take effective action to prevent such violence may be liable for injuries that result. Yet failure to accommodate employees with mental disabilities may violate the ADA.

The ADA provides a way to resolve this tension, but it is sometimes difficult to apply in practice. The ADA provides that an employer's obligation to reasonably accommodate employee disabilities does not require actions that pose a direct threat to the health and safety of others. The term "direct threat" means a significant risk of substantial harm that cannot be eliminated or reduced by reasonable accommodation. Such determinations must be individualized and based on current medical and other objective evidence.

When an employee becomes violent in the workplace or engages in misconduct that suggests a significant risk of violence, the employer may take appropriate preventative action, including discharging the employee, despite the existence of a disability. An employer may discipline an employee with a disability for engaging in misconduct if it would impose the same discipline on an employee without a disability. In recent cases, courts have upheld employee discharges where the employees have engaged in such inappropriate conduct. In one case, an employee who had previously been disciplined for disruptions and abusive behavior brought a stun gun and mace to work. In another case, an employee brought a loaded firearm onto company premises. In both cases the employees claimed that they suffered from disabilities and requested reasonable accommodations, but courts held that the employer was required to provide no further accommodation because the threat to safety justified discharge. But where the employer merely suspects that the employee may have a tendency toward violence and there is no historical or medical evidence to substantiate that suspicion, the ADA will protect an employee with a mental disability.

See **Workplace violence** in the companion **Survival Guide**.

State employers and the ADA

Recently courts have addressed whether the ADA effectively abrogates state immunity under the 11th Amendment to the Constitution. Although this issue has not been resolved by the United States Supreme Court, several appellate courts have held that the ADA is not applicable to state employers, and that only state anti-discrimination laws apply. The Supreme Court has held that the Age Discrimination in Employment Act is not applicable to state employers because congress lacked power to invalidate the states' 11th Amendment immunity. Thus far this has only been applied in cases where the state was the employer (for example, state department of transportation, state department of corrections or state board of regents). See Chapter 11, **Age discrimination**.

Practical pointers

An employer **MAY**:

- Require disabled employees to comply with attendance policies applied to non-disabled employees, unless variance from the policy would be a reasonable accommodation.

- Require an employee seeking an accommodation to undergo a medical examination to assist in the assessment of what, if any, accommodation is required.

- Hire the most qualified candidate for the job without giving preference to disabled applicants.

- Require disabled employees, with reasonable accommodations if necessary, to meet the same standards of production, safety and performance as non-disabled employees.

- Refuse to provide an accommodation to a disabled employee which would conflict with an established seniority system.

- Discipline an employee with a disability who cannot meet conduct or production standards if no effective reasonable accommodation exists.

- Select an accommodation that is not the employee's first choice, provided the accommodation is effective.

- Ask an applicant whether he is able to perform the essential functions of the job (for example, lifting 50 pounds) with or without reasonable accommodation.

- Ask an applicant with a known disability to demonstrate or describe how she would perform an essential function of the job.

- Ask an applicant if she can meet the company's attendance policy.

Practical pointers

An employer **MAY NOT**:

- Require employment applicants to undergo physical examinations before an offer of employment has been made.

- Discharge an employee upon learning that he or she is infected with HIV.

- Refuse to hire an applicant whose spouse suffers from cancer based on the fear of dependent insurance claims.

- Fail to make a pre-employment test site accessible to an applicant who needs a wheelchair.

- Inquire about specific disabilities on job applications.

- Inquire whether a job applicant has ever received psychiatric care.

- Refuse to accommodate an employee's known disability because the employee has not expressly requested accommodation.

- Discharge an employee who is no longer able to perform the essential functions of the position because of a disability where the employer has a vacant position for which the employee is qualified.

- Inquire about an applicant's past workers' compensation history.

- Ask an applicant how many days he absent in his prior job because of illness or disability.

Chapter 13

Family and Medical Leave Act

The Family and Medical Leave Act of 1993 (FMLA) requires employers to grant employees unpaid leaves of absence with job protection and no loss of service for family-related matters such as childbirth or a serious health condition.

Eligibility

A person seeking FMLA leave must:

- be an employee (management or non-management)

  and

- have been employed for a total of at least 12 months (not necessarily consecutively)

  and

- have worked at least 1,250 hours during the 12 months before commencement of the leave

  and

- be employed at a location where the employer employs at least 50 employees within a 75 mile radius.

Amount of and reasons for leave

Leave is limited to 12 weeks during a 12-month period for any of the following reasons:

- the birth and care of a child of the employee

- the adoption of a child by the employee or acceptance of a child for foster care

- the care of a spouse, child (who is under 18 years of age or incapable of self-care due to a disability), or parent (not parent-in-law) with a serious health condition (includes providing psychological comfort or reassurance)

- the employee's own serious health condition that renders the employee unable to perform his or her job.

Determination of the 12-month period

Employers may choose any one of four methods for determining the 12-month period:

- calendar year

- any fixed 12-month "leave year," such as a year starting on the employee's anniversary date

- the 12-month period measured forward from the date the employee's first FMLA leave begins

- a "rolling" 12-month period measured backward from the date the employee uses any FMLA leave.

An employer's FMLA policy must specify which of these methods will be used. Generally, option 4 is recommended because it minimizes an employee's time away from work.

Leave for the birth, adoption or foster care of a child must be completed within one year after the date of birth, adoption or foster placement.

Serious health condition

"Serious health condition" is an illness, injury, impairment, or physical or mental condition that requires or results in:

- an overnight stay in a hospital, hospice, or residential medical-care facility, or incapacity connected with that stay

  or

- inability to work, attend school, or perform other regular daily activities that is:

  - more than 3 consecutive calendar days in duration and involves two or more treatments under the supervision of a health care provider, or one treatment by a health care provider that results in a regimen of continuing treatment under the supervision of a health care provider

    or

  - due to pregnancy (of any duration)

    or

- due to a chronic condition that requires periodic treatments over an extended period of time and may cause episodic rather than a continuing period of incapacity (for example, asthma, diabetes, or epilepsy)

  or

- permanent or long-term due to a condition that requires the continuing supervision of a health care provider (for example, Alzheimer's or terminal stages of a disease)

  or

- any period of absence to receive multiple treatments under the supervision of a health care provider either for restorative surgery after an accident or injury, or for a condition that would likely result in a period of incapacity of more than 3 consecutive calendar days in the absence of treatment, such as cancer (chemotherapy, radiation, etc.) or kidney diseases (dialysis, etc.).

Examples of conditions that are not "serious medical conditions" include the common cold, the flu, earaches, upset stomach, minor ulcers, headaches other than migraine, routine dental problems, and similar afflictions.

Generally, FMLA leave may be taken for treatment of substance abuse by a health care provider. Absence caused by the employee's use of the substance, rather than treatment, does not qualify for FMLA leave.

Where husband and wife are both company employees

A husband and wife are permitted to take only a combined total of 12 weeks of leave during a 12-month period if the leave is for the birth and care of a child or the placement of a child for adoption or foster care.

Reduced or intermittent leave

Leave based upon the serious health condition of the employee or the employee's family member may be intermittent or on a reduced schedule if it is medically necessary. "Intermittent leave" is leave of one hour or more taken during any nonconsecutive time period (for example, one week on, one week off). "Reduced leave" is leave that is taken by reducing the employee's normal working hours (for example, from eight hours to four hours per day).

An employer may alter an employee's existing job (while maintaining existing pay and benefits) or may temporarily transfer the employee to a different position with equivalent pay and benefits to lessen the impact of intermittent or reduced leave on the employer's operations.

Procedures for leave

Notice

An employee must provide an employer with 30 calendar days advance notice prior to the expected start of the leave. If 30 days advance notice is not possible, the employee must provide the employer with as much advance notice as possible, ordinarily within one or two business days of the date that the need for leave becomes known to the employee. The employer may delay the start of the leave to the extent of any required notice period. If the employee is physically or mentally unable to notify the employer, a member of the employee's family or other representative must do so on the employee's behalf.

Verification

The employer may require the employee to provide a health care provider's certification if leave is required due to a serious health condition. The completed certification must be submitted by the employee to the employer within 15 calendar days after the employer requests it. The 8th Circuit Court of Appeals recently ruled that an employer who does not request medical certification forgoes the right to challenge whether the employee has a serious health condition.

Approval of the leave

An employer ordinarily must notify an employee whether the request has been granted within 2 business days of learning from information provided by the employee the reason for the request. This preliminary notice becomes final unless revoked in writing by the employer and, if necessary, replaced with another notification within 2 business days. An employer may revoke the preliminary notice if the employee's medical certification does not support the stated reason for the leave or if no certification is provided. A recent decision of the 8th Circuit Court of Appeals has also held that if the employer fails to notify an employee that it has designated his or her leave as FMLA leave, the leave still counts against the employee's 12-month allotment if other qualifying factors are met.

Retrospective designation

An employer may designate an employee's leave as FMLA leave after the employee has returned to work if:

- the employer knows the reason for the leave but is waiting for the requested medical certification, as long as the employer preliminarily designated the leave as FMLA leave as set forth above

    or

- the employee is absent for a FMLA reason and the employer does not learn the reason for the absence until after the employee's return to work, as long as the leave is designated within 2 business days of learning the reason for the absence and notice is given to the employee.

Substitution of paid leave

The employer may require an employee to substitute accrued vacation, sick or other paid personal time for unpaid FMLA leave. Disability and worker's compensation leaves also may run at the same time as unpaid FMLA leave. For example, an employee with 2 weeks accrued vacation and short-term disability benefits who requests 12 weeks FMLA leave for the birth and care of his or her child is entitled to a maximum of 12 weeks leave, the first six of which may be paid under the employer's short-term disability policy (for the employee's own disability due to childbirth), the seventh and eighth of which may be paid under the employer's vacation policy, and the ninth through the twelfth of which are unpaid.

Release for work

The employer may require that the employee provide medical certification that he or she is able to return to work when the leave is based upon the employee's own serious health condition.

Status of employee benefits during leave of absence

Unless the employee declares an intent not to return to work following the leave, an employer must maintain and pay for group health insurance coverage (including dependent coverage) during the period of an FMLA leave under the same terms and conditions as if the employee had continued to work. An employer may require an employee to pay his or her share of the premium in any of the following ways:

- payment at the same time as it would be if by payroll deduction

- payment on the same schedule as payments made under COBRA

- prepayment according to a cafeteria or flexible benefits plan at the employee's option

- the employer's existing rules for payment by employees on "leave without pay," provided that such rules do not require prepayment (that is, prior to the commencement of the leave) of the premiums that will become due during a period of unpaid FMLA leave or payment of higher premiums than if the employee had continued to work instead of taking leave

- another system voluntarily agreed to between the employer and the employee, which may include prepayment of premiums (for example, through increased deductions when the need for FMLA is foreseeable).

An employer must provide advance written notice of the method by which the employee must make payment.

Employees who do not comply with premium payment obligations during the leave period may be dropped from plan coverage until the leave period terminates and they return to work.

An employer is not obligated to maintain life insurance or other benefits, such as dental insurance, long-term disability, and profit sharing, during the leave period, so long as it does not maintain these benefits during other types of unpaid leave.

If an employee informs an employer that he or she has decided not to return to work from the leave or fails to return to work upon completion of the leave, an employer may recover from the employee the premiums it paid during the leave to maintain the employee's group health insurance coverage. However, the employer may not recover the premiums if the employee does not return to work due to the recurrence or onset of a serious health condition, or for other reasons beyond the employee's control.

Reinstatement at the conclusion of the leave

An employee must be reinstated to the same position that he or she would have held had he or she not taken leave or to an equivalent position with equivalent benefits, pay and other terms and conditions of employment. However, if the employee would no longer be employed had he or she not taken leave (for example, because of a job elimination or reduction-in-force) the employee is not entitled to reinstatement.

"Key" employees

A "key" employee is a salaried employee who is among the highest paid 10% of employees within 75 miles of the work site.

An employer may refuse to reinstate a "key" employee after FMLA leave, if reinstating that employee would cause substantial and grievous economic injury to its operations. However, the employer must have notified the employee of his or her status as a "key" employee at the time of the request for FMLA leave. Additionally, the employer must have notified the employee of its decision not to reinstate the employee and the reasons for the decision as soon as possible after the decision is made.

Application of state and local laws

An employer must comply with state and local laws that provide greater family or medical leave rights than the FMLA.

Enforcement and remedies for violations

FMLA is enforced by the U.S. Labor Department's Employment Standards Administration, Wage and Hour Division. The Department may file a lawsuit in court to require compliance. An employee may also bring a private civil suit against an employer for violations. Available remedies for violations include:

- reinstatement

- backpay and benefits

- other out-of-pocket losses (for example, costs of care)

- liquidated damages

- attorneys' fees and costs.

Wage and hour implications

Salaried executive, administrative, and professional employees who meet the Fair Labor Standards Act (FLSA) criteria for exemption from minimum wage and overtime requirements do not lose their FLSA-exempt status by using unpaid FMLA leave on an intermittent or reduced schedule basis. Employers may make deductions from an employee's salary for any hours taken as intermittent or reduced FMLA leave within a workweek without affecting the exempt status of the employee.

No-fault attendance policies

FMLA-qualifying absences cannot be counted against an employee under a no-fault attendance policy. Similarly, FMLA-qualifying absences cannot be counted against an employee for purposes of determining his or her eligibility for a perfect attendance bonus or award.

FMLA policies

An employer is required to have a written FMLA policy if it has a handbook, policy manual or collective bargaining agreement. Failure to include such a policy may result in an employer losing rights under the FMLA, including the right to require medical certifications of "serious health conditions."

If an employer has no written policies, it is not required to have a written FMLA policy.

Commonly asked questions and answers

Q. Must an employee ask specifically for FMLA leave to be entitled to it?

A. No. If an employee requests leave simply because he or she is "sick," the employer is obliged to ask sufficient follow-up questions to determine if the employee's illness is a "serious medical condition."

Q. May an employer "charge" an employee's FMLA leave account for time off taken by the employee even if the employee does not ask for FMLA leave?

A. Yes, if the employer learns that the time off was used for an FMLA purpose, and if the employer notifies the employee, in writing, that the time off is being charged as FMLA leave.

Q. Does workers' compensation leave count against an employee's FMLA leave entitlement?

A. It may. FMLA leave and workers' compensation leave may run at the same time, provided the reason for the absence is due to a qualifying serious injury or illness.

Q. Do the 1,250 hours that an employee must work to be eligible for FMLA coverage include paid leave time or other absences from work?

A. No. The 1,250 hours include only those hours actually worked for the employer. Paid leave and unpaid leave, including FMLA leave, are not included.

Q. Under what circumstances may an employer deny an employee leave or reinstatement without violating the FMLA?

A. Employers may refuse to reinstate a "key" employee under the circumstances described on page 114, **Reinstatement at the conclusion of the leave**.

Employers are not required to continue FMLA benefits or reinstate employees who would have been laid off or otherwise had their employment terminated had they continued to work during the FMLA leave period.

Employees who give unequivocal notice that they do not intend to return to work lose their entitlement to FMLA leave.

Employees who are unable to return to work and have exhausted their 12 weeks of FMLA leave during the designated 12-month period no longer have the FMLA protections of leave or job restoration.

Under certain circumstances, employers who advise employees experiencing a serious health condition that they will require a medical certificate of fitness for duty to return to work may deny reinstatement to an employee who fails to provide the certification or may delay reinstatement until the certification is submitted.

Q. May an employer who allows employees a certain number of absences according to a "no fault" attendance policy count FMLA leave against an employee under the policy?

A. No. FMLA covered absences may not be counted as absences under a "no fault" attendance policy and may not otherwise be used as a basis for discipline.

Q. May an employer decide that an employee who takes FMLA leave is ineligible for a bonus for perfect attendance?

A. No. To the extent an employee who takes an FMLA leave otherwise meets the requirements for an attendance bonus program, the employee continues to be qualified for the bonus.

Chapter 14

Protection of union-related activities

Activities protected

The Labor Management Relations Act (LMRA) prohibits employment discrimination based on employees' efforts to organize, support or join labor unions or to work together to obtain changes in terms and conditions of employment. The LMRA also forbids employment discrimination against employees who choose not to participate in union-related activities. The LMRA applies to all private sector employers. Comparable state laws apply to most public employers.

How employees are protected

The National Labor Relations Board enforces employees' rights under the LMRA. The Board:

- conducts elections to determine whether employees wish to be represented and requires employers and labor organizations to abide by the results

- investigates charges that employers or unions have wrongfully interfered with the exercise of rights under the LMRA

- orders employers or unions to cease violating the law and to rehire, pay lost wages and benefits, or provide other relief to employees who have been illegally prevented from exercising their rights, coerced or threatened not to exercise their rights, or discriminated against for having joined a labor organization

- requires employers and unions to bargain in good faith

- requires employers and unions to notify employees of their rights and to promise not to interfere with the exercise of those rights

- seeks to have its orders enforced by courts.

What kinds of employer actions discriminate against employees

Employment discrimination prohibited by the LMRA is adverse action taken by an employer against an employee because the employee exercised a right under the LMRA. Examples of unlawful discrimination include:

- terminating an employee because the employee supported a union organizing drive

- disciplining an employee who asked for a union representative to be present at an interview when the employee had a reasonable belief that the interview might result in disciplinary action

- refusing an employee's request to have a union representative present when the employee reasonably believes that an interview or interrogation might result in disciplining action. In the Epilepsy Foundation of Ohio, the Board extended this principle to non-union employees who request the presence of a co-worker during an investigative interview, so long as the employee reasonably believes that the interview may result in disciplinary action

- disciplining an employee for talking about the union during non-working hours in non-work areas (for example, before work in the company parking lot)

- closing and then relocating a plant because the employees at the first location elected to be represented by a union

- terminating employees because they commenced a lawful strike

- disciplining two or more non-supervisory employees who are not represented by a union but who together request changes in their terms or conditions of employment

- disciplining employees for talking to each other about salaries or wages. The Sixth U.S. Circuit Court of Appeals recently reaffirmed this principle in **NLRB v. Main Street Terrace Care Center**, which struck down as unlawful an employer's work rule that prohibited employees, in a non-unionized workforce, from communicating with each other about wages.

Commonly asked questions and answers

Q. May an employer discipline an employee for campaigning for union representation?

A. No. Employees have the right to seek union representation and so cannot be disciplined for supporting a union. However, if the employee is ignoring his or her job duties to campaign during work hours, this may be cause for discipline.

Q. May an employer discipline an employee who is also a representative of the union (often called a union steward)?

A. Yes. However, the employer must be prepared to prove that the employee was disciplined for specific misconduct, the same as other employees, and not because of his or her union activities or position with the union.

Q. Does an employee have the right to stop working if he or she believes that the job is unsafe?

A. Perhaps. The Labor Management Relations Act provides that an employee in good faith may stop working because of "abnormally" dangerous conditions without being regarded as on strike. If the employee is not on strike, he may not be disciplined for violating a no-strike agreement. To receive this protection, the employee's assessment of the situation must be:

- in good faith

  and

- reasonable (that is, a reasonable employee with the same skills and experience would regard the conditions as abnormally dangerous compared to normal working conditions).

Q. May an employer discipline an employee who refuses to pay full union dues?

A. No. Employers may not discipline or discriminate against employees who refuse to pay more than an equal share of the union's cost of providing collective bargaining and contract-enforcement services to the bargaining unit.

Chapter 15

Discrimination based on safety activities

The Occupational Safety and Health Act (OSHA) and the 1994 Commercial Motor Vehicle Safety Amendments to the Surface Transportation Assistance Act both prohibit discrimination against employees because of safety-related activity.

The Occupational Safety and Health Act (OSHA)

OSHA prohibits employers from discriminating against an employee for:

- filing a complaint under OSHA or "related to" OSHA

- discussing safety-related matters with OSHA investigators

- complaining to management about safety-related issues

- filing safety grievances

- refusing to perform abnormally dangerous work at hours when OSHA is not available to receive and investigate a complaint

- testifying in an OSHA-related proceeding

- exercising any rights provided by OSHA.

An employee's safety complaint does not need to be based on actual hazards or violations of the law to be protected. An employee is protected as long as the complaint is related to a safety issue.

Example
An employee repeatedly complains that fumes in the workplace are making him dizzy. The employer has workplace air tested. The tests show no fumes. It is unlawful for the employer to discipline the employee for making false complaints.

Time limits

A charge of discrimination under OSHA must be received by the U.S. Department of Labor within 30 days after the discriminatory action has been taken. The Department is supposed to inform the complaining employee of its findings within 90 days after receipt of the complaint. However, the Department routinely exceeds the time limit for investigations.

Procedures

Each discrimination complaint will be assigned for investigation to a Compliance Safety and Health Officer (CSHO) of the Department of Labor. The CSHO will interview witnesses and consider other evidence offered by the employer and the employee. The CSHO may subpoena witnesses to give statements under oath and to produce relevant documents.

If the CSHO concludes that illegal discrimination has occurred, the Department of Labor may file suit against the employer to recover lost wages and re-employment. Neither OSHA nor the Department of Labor may impose penalties on the employer directly. Rather, the Department must file suit in federal court for the purpose of enforcing its recommended award. Only if the Department wins in federal court will the employer be required to pay the employee backpay or reinstate him. The employee may not file suit on his own, even in cases where the Department decides not to file a suit.

States with their own OSHA plans

The U.S. Department of Labor generally retains jurisdiction to enforce the anti-discrimination provisions of OSHA.

Among the 21 states with approved state plans, some provide independent procedures for handling employee complaints of discrimination; in others, the state will be assigned the responsibility for investigation and in other states the Department of Labor (DOL) handles the cases (see table on page 125).

	State approved plan			Federal plan
	State handles employee complaints	State responsible for investigation	DOL handles employee complaints	
Alabama				x
Alaska	x			
Arizona			x	
Arkansas				x
California	x			
Colorado				x
Connecticut				x
Delaware				x
Florida				x
Georgia				x
Hawaii	x			
Idaho				x
Illinois				x
Indiana	x			
Iowa	x			
Kansas				x
Kentucky		x		
Louisiana				x
Maine				x
Maryland	x			
Massachusetts				x
Michigan			x	
Minnesota	x			
Mississippi				x
Missouri				x
Montana				x
Nebraska				x
Nevada			x	
New Hampshire				x
New Jersey				x
New Mexico			x	
New York				x
North Carolina			x	
North Dakota				x
Ohio				x
Oklahoma				x
Oregon			x	
Pennsylvania				x
Rhode Island				x
South Carolina		x		
South Dakota				x
Tennessee		x		
Texas				x
Utah			x	
Vermont			x	
Virginia		x		
Washington			x	
West Virginia				x
Wisconsin				x
Wyoming		x		

Commercial motor vehicle safety

The 1994 Commercial Motor Vehicle Safety Amendments to the Surface Transportation Assistance Act prohibit certain forms of discrimination against drivers of commercial motor vehicles. Drivers of commercial motor vehicles are protected against employment discrimination that is based on the following activities:

- filing safety complaints related to an alleged violation of a commercial motor vehicle safety regulation or order

- testifying in proceedings related to such complaints

- refusing to operate a vehicle because, either:

  - the operation violates a safety or health regulation, standard or order

    or

  - the prospect of operating the vehicle creates a "reasonable" apprehension of serious injury to the employee or to the public because of an "unsafe" condition of the vehicle.

Protected employees

The law protects drivers of commercial vehicles. Commercial motor vehicles are vehicles with a gross vehicle weight of at least 10,000 pounds, vehicles used to transport more than 10 persons including the driver, or vehicles used to transport hazardous materials.

Procedures

An employee who believes that he or she has suffered discriminatory treatment may file a complaint with the Department of Labor within 180 days of the alleged discrimination. A CSHO will then investigate the case and recommend action. After the complaint is filed, the Department must make a preliminary finding either that the employer has discriminated against the employee or that the complaint is without merit. The losing party then has 30 days in which to request a formal hearing of the issues. If a hearing is requested, the Secretary of Labor must hold a hearing, review the results and issue a final order. The Secretary's order ultimately may be appealed to the appropriate Court of Appeals.

Preliminary orders

This law incorporates a feature not found in other laws against employment discrimination. An employer who is believed by the Department of Labor to have committed discrimination in violation of this law may be ordered to reinstate the employee with back pay at that point, prior to conclusion of a formal hearing and formal finding by the Secretary of Labor.

Commonly asked questions and answers

Q. May an employer discipline an employee who files a complaint with OSHA?

A. An employer may not discipline an employee for filing a complaint with OSHA. However, the employer continues to be able to discipline the employee for misconduct unrelated to filing the complaint. The employer must be prepared to show that the misconduct was the reason for the discipline, not the complaint.

Q. Is it illegal to fire or discipline an employee who violates safety rules?

A. No. It is not unlawful to discipline an employee for violating safety rules. In fact, OSHA **requires** an employer to enforce safety rules with disciplinary action severe enough to obtain compliance.

Q. What happens if the employee has filed charges with other agencies or under a collective bargaining agreement?

A. The Department of Labor has a policy (published as a regulation) to defer its own action pending the results of other such proceedings. It will not necessarily abide by the results of the other agencies, however.

Q. When will an employee be protected in refusing work assignments that he or she regards as unsafe?

A. The applicable Department of Labor regulation (29 CFR 1977.12(b)(2)) describes five elements that must exist: the employee must be "reasonable" in refusing the assignment (that is, that any reasonable person in the employee's situation would be apprehensive); the employee must refuse in good faith because of safety considerations and not for some other reason (such as to force the employer to pay more money for the job); the danger must be one that poses the risk of death or serious physical harm; the employee must have notified the employer of the risk and have been unable to persuade the employer to take action; and the situation must arise when there is insufficient time to invoke the safety complaint procedures provided by OSHA. Under these circumstances, the employee would be protected from discrimination for lodging a complaint under OSHA. Generally speaking, the rule is intended to cover situations where the employee has no realistic option other than to undertake a job that he sees as being abnormally dangerous, at a time when he is unable to call the Department of Labor to intervene.

Chapter 16

Military status discrimination

Employment discrimination against veterans is prohibited by both the Uniformed Services Employment and Reemployment Rights Act of 1994 (USERRA) and the Vietnam Era Veterans' Readjustment Assistance Act of 1974 (VEVRAA). USERRA applies to all employers, both public and private. VEVRAA applies to federal employers, federal contractors and recipients of federal assistance.

Uniformed Services Employment and Reemployment Rights Act (USERRA)

The Uniformed Services Employment and Reemployment Rights Act of 1994 (USERRA) prohibits discrimination against persons because of their service in the uniformed services. Uniformed services include:

- the Armed Forces

- the Army National Guard and the Air National Guard

- the commissioned corps of the Public Health Service

- any other category designated by the President in time of war or emergency.

USERRA covers voluntary or involuntary service and includes time spent in:

- active duty

- inactive duty training

- full-time National Guard duty

- an examination to determine fitness for such duty.

Prohibited discrimination

USERRA prohibits employers from denying employment, reemployment, retention in employment, promotions or any other employment benefit because of service in the uniformed services.

Persons who have received dishonorable discharges or were separated from the uniformed service under other than honorable conditions are not protected by USERRA.

Reemployment rights for veterans

An employee absent from work because of service in the uniformed services is entitled to reemployment if:

- the employee has given either written or oral advance notice of service to the employer, unless giving notice is prevented by military necessity or is otherwise impossible

- the cumulative length of all absences because of service does not exceed 5 years, unless the employee is required or ordered to remain in service beyond 5 years

- depending on the length of service (see chart on page 131), the employee reports to or submits an application for reemployment to the employer. Employers may require employees to submit documentation that their application is timely, that they have not exceeded their service limitations and that their separation from the uniformed service was under honorable conditions.

Length of service	Employee obligations
Less than 31 days or absence for take a physical examination.	Must report to the employer not later than the beginning of the first regularly scheduled work period of the first full calender day following the completion of service and the expiration of 8 hours after a period allowing for safe transportation.
More than 30 days but less than 181 days.	Must submit an application for reemployment within 14 days after the completion of service (this may be extended if the employee cannot submit the application for reasons that are not the employee's fault.)
More than 180 days.	Must submit an application for reemployment within 90 days after the completion of service.

If an employee is hospitalized or convalescing from an illness or injury related to his or her period of service, the employee must report to the employer or submit an application once the recovery period has ended. The recovery period may not exceed 2 years unless circumstances beyond the employee's control make reporting or applying within 2 years impossible or unreasonable.

Exceptions to the right of reemployment

An employer is not required to reemploy an employee upon completion of uniformed service if the employer proves any one of the following:

- the employer's circumstances have so changed as to make reemployment impossible or unreasonable. For example, if an employer has closed the plant at which the employee formerly worked, reemployment would not be required.

- the initial employment was for a brief, nonrecurrent period with no reasonable expectation that it would continue indefinitely or for a significant period. For example, if an employer hires extra employees only for the holiday shopping rush, reemployment would not be required.

- the employee was disabled during the period of service and is no longer qualified to resume his or her prior position even with reasonable accommodation, and additional training or effort by the employer would impose an undue hardship.

- the employee was discharged from service under less than honorable conditions.

Positions upon reemployment

Service less than 91 days

An employee who has served for 90 days or less is entitled to the position that he or she would have held had the employee remained continuously employed, assuming he or she is qualified for that job. If the employee is unable to become qualified after reasonable efforts by the employer, then he or she must be returned to the position held when he or she commenced service.

Service over 90 days

An employee who served more than 90 days must be placed in the position that he or she would have held if he or she had remained continuously employed, or a position of like seniority, status and pay. However, if the employee is not qualified for the position, then he or she must be reinstated in the position held when the service began, or one with like seniority, status and pay.

Non-qualified disabled employees

If an employee is not qualified to perform the duties of the position to which he or she is entitled because of a disability incurred or aggravated during service, then the employee must be placed in a position of equivalent seniority, status or pay if the employee can perform the duties of the position.

Non-qualified, non-disabled employees

If an employee is not qualified to perform the duties of the position to which he or she is entitled for any reason other than disability and cannot become qualified with reasonable effort, then he or she must be placed in any other position with lesser status and pay which he or she is qualified to perform and must be given full seniority.

Employment benefits

Seniority-based employment benefits

Upon reemployment, employees are entitled to all of the seniority-based employee benefits they had when their uniformed service began plus any additional benefits they would have accrued had they remained continuously employed. For example, if vacations are determined by the number of years of service, the period spent in uniformed service would count in determining the number of vacation days employees receive upon their return.

Non-seniority-based employment benefits

Employees are entitled to benefits not determined by seniority according to the employer's general policy for employees who are on leaves of absence.

Employees may choose, but cannot be required, to use accrued vacation or similar leave with pay during the period of uniformed service.

Health care benefits

Under USERRA, all health care plans are required to provide COBRA-type coverage for up to 18 months during a period of uniformed service. Employees or dependents who elect this coverage may be required to pay a premium identical to COBRA. However, for leaves of less than 31 days, employees may be charged only the normal employee contribution.

Upon reemployment, employees and their dependents are entitled to restoration of the coverage they had prior to their uniformed service leave. Employers are prohibited from imposing exclusions and waiting periods (such as for preexisting conditions) except for injuries or illnesses found to be service-related by the Veterans' Administration.

Pension benefits

USERRA obligates employers to credit employees with years of service while on uniformed service leave and to fund both defined benefit and defined contribution plans for those years. Contributions to defined contribution plans are based upon the rate of pay that employees would have received for that period or for the employees' average compensation during the twelve months preceding the period of service. Employees are not, however, entitled to earnings or forfeitures that would have been added to their accounts during the leave.

Employees must also be allowed to make up elective deferrals and required employee contributions, and, if they do, the employer must make any matching contributions required by the plan. Employees have 3 times the length of their leave (a maximum of 5 years) to make these contributions.

Termination of employment

USERRA limits employers' ability to terminate employees after reemployment from uniformed service. Employees reemployed after serving more than 180 days cannot be discharged, except for cause, within 1 year of reemployment. Employees who served for more than 30 days but less than 181 days cannot be discharged, except for cause, within 180 days after reemployment.

VEVRAA

The Vietnam Era Veterans' Readjustment Assistance Act of 1974 (VEVRAA) protects qualified disabled veterans and veterans of the Vietnam era from discrimination in employment and requires affirmative action to ensure nondiscrimination for persons with protected veteran status. VEVRAA applies to federal contractors and subcontractors. For further information regarding federal contractors' obligations to veterans, see Chapter 18, **Affirmative action**.

State law

At least one state also prohibits discrimination against persons who have served in the uniformed services. Illinois, for example, prohibits discrimination in employment against persons who have received an unfavorable military discharge. Under Illinois law, an unfavorable military discharge is one which is less than honorable, but not dishonorable.

Practical pointers

An employer **MAY**:

- Refuse to reinstate an employee who received a dishonorable discharge.

- Allow an employee to use vacation time when taking leave to serve in the uniformed services.

- Require an employee to submit documentation to establish that his or her application for reemployment is timely, that he or she has not exceeded the length of service limitations, or that his or her separation from service was honorable.

- Refuse to reinstate an employee if circumstances have changed to make reinstatement unreasonable, such as a reduction in force that would have encompassed the employee's job.

- Provide a reinstated employee with non-seniority based benefits according to the employer's policy for employees who take leaves of absence.

Practical pointers

An employer **MAY NOT**:

- Refuse to hire an applicant because of his or her prior uniformed service.

- Discharge an employee who will be absent from work for 5 years or less due to uniformed service.

- Discharge an employee after reemployment from uniformed service, except for just cause, within a set time (depending on length of service) after reemployment.

- Require an employee to use vacation time while on uniformed service leave.

- Impose exclusions or waiting periods for health care benefits upon reemployment, except for an employee who has sustained service-related injuries.

- Deny a reemployed employee seniority-based benefits that would have accrued had he or she remained employed.

Chapter 17

Discrimination in employee benefits

In addition to the traditional prohibitions against discrimination discussed elsewhere in this guide, the law prohibits discrimination in the provision of employee benefits. First, the Employee Retirement Income Security Act of 1974 (ERISA) prohibits discrimination against a plan participant or beneficiary for either exercising benefit rights or for the purpose of interfering with the attainment of benefit rights. Second, the Internal Revenue Code limits discrimination in favor of highly compensated employees in the provision of certain tax-qualified benefits. Finally, the traditional discrimination laws prohibit discrimination against a plan participant or beneficiary on the basis of disability, age or pregnancy.

Interference with benefit rights

Section 510 of ERISA makes it unlawful for a person to discharge, fine, suspend, expel, discipline or discriminate against a benefit plan participant or beneficiary if the action is taken:

- in retaliation for exercising benefit rights

- for the purpose of interfering with the attainment of a benefit right

    or

- in retaliation for testifying, preparing to testify or giving information in a proceeding related to ERISA.

This type of discrimination can arise in a number of contexts.

Chronic or serious illness

An employer learns that an employee or an employee's dependent has a chronic or serious illness that is likely to increase health insurance costs or make insurance unavailable to other employees.

- **Under these circumstances, an employer may:**

    - limit benefit plan coverage in ways that do not relate to a specific disease or disability such as instituting lifetime benefit maximums, co-payments or deductibles for all employees

    - change the plan design to less costly alternatives such as an HMO or a community-rated policy

    - change insurance policies or carriers

    - limit treatment to particular providers or facilities that are designated by the plan to treat such illnesses or perform transplants

    - discharge the employee if, due to the illness, the employee can no longer perform the essential functions of the job or for other legitimate reasons

- **An employer may not:**

    - discharge the employee to keep the employee (or the employee's dependent) from submitting expensive health claims to the benefit plan

    - reduce hours of work to make the employee (or the employee's dependent) ineligible for plan coverage

    - coerce, intimidate or threaten the employee to force the employee to drop plan coverage.

Layoffs, reductions in force and plant closings

An employer is considering layoffs, job eliminations or plant closings.

- **Under these circumstances, an employer may:**

    - consider overall benefit costs or the cost of shutdown benefits in determining whether to reduce the workforce

    - offer benefit enhancements as an incentive for employees to resign voluntarily

    - offer benefit enhancements in exchange for a release of claims against the employer (see page 83, **Older Workers Benefit Protection Act of 1990**)

- offer enhancements only to particular job classes, departments or plants, provided that the enhancement does not disproportionately exclude protected minorities, women or older employees

- lay off employees under a bona fide union seniority agreement regardless of benefit impact.

- **An employer may not:**

  - lay off employees or close a plant solely to prevent employees from attaining a nonforfeitable right in their pensions (to prevent employees from "vesting")

  - lay off employees solely to prevent them from becoming eligible for early retirement subsidies or benefit enhancements

  - schedule the timing of layoffs and recalls for the purpose of preventing employees from earning pension credit while on layoff

  - select individual employees for layoff because the employee or an employee's dependent has a costly medical condition

  - fail to disclose benefit programs or exit incentives that are under serious consideration in response to employee inquiries.

Note that some cases have held that employers must affirmatively disclose benefit programs that are under serious consideration even if employees fail to request such information.

Sales of facilities or subsidiaries

Most courts have rejected employees' claims that an employer violates section 510 of ERISA by selling the facility or subsidiary where they work. Thus:

- employers are not required to make purchasers adopt and continue benefit plans

- employers generally are not required to vest employees in their benefits upon a sale. However, if a qualified pension or profit sharing plan is terminated in conjunction with a sale, ERISA requires, among other things, that all pensions become immediately vested. Also, if a substantial number of plan participants are terminated as a result of a sale or if employer contributions are significantly reduced, these situations could give rise to a partial plan termination requiring the pensions of terminated participants to be immediately vested

- severance pay plans may be designed to deny severance to individuals who are subsequently employed by the purchaser

- some courts have held that benefit plans, such as severance programs may be terminated or amended prior to a sale to avoid benefit liability.

Discrimination in favor of highly compensated employees

The Internal Revenue Code of 1986 includes non-discrimination rules that certain benefit plans must meet to receive favorable tax treatment. Favorable tax treatment for the employee may include the deferral of income tax on the benefit (and accumulated interest) until retirement or some other future date, while the employer may qualify for an immediate tax deduction. These rules may require such plans to:

- provide benefits proportionately between highly compensated and non-highly compensated employees

  and

- provide benefits on the same basis to all employees equally, unless there is a legitimate business reason for denying benefits to employees in different job classifications, functions, departments, divisions or subsidiaries.

A highly compensated employee is an employee who:

- was a 5% owner at any time during the year or the preceding year

  or

- for the preceding year had compensation in excess of $80,000 and, if the employer elects, was in the top paid 20% of employees.

Unlike traditional non-discrimination legislation, discrimination based on compensation or job difference is not flatly prohibited. An employer may discriminate if it is willing to forego the favorable tax treatment that certain benefits provide.

When employers distinguish between employees based on compensation, different and specific numerical tests apply to various types of benefits to determine whether the particular benefit scheme is discriminatory. When employers distinguish between employees in different job classifications, functions, departments, divisions or subsidiaries, the IRS provides guidelines to determine whether the exclusion of some groups of employees is reasonable.

Finally, certain types of welfare benefits, such as benefits funded through an employer's general assets, which are not tax-qualified, are not subject to these rules. For welfare benefits that are subject to these rules, such as cafeteria plans, fringe benefit plans and self-funded welfare plans, the technical details of the tests are similar to those for qualified pension plans.

Welfare benefits and payroll practices

Management has complete discretion in deciding whether to offer certain welfare and payroll practice benefits to particular employees, as long as such welfare plans are paid from the general assets of an employer and not a trust fund. Examples of welfare benefits that are paid from employer's general assets may include short-term disability payments, severance pay, vacation pay and sick pay. In short, there are no rules that require an employer to provide these benefits to all employees on an equal basis.

Medical and dental insurance

Management also has discretion in providing medical and dental benefits as long as those benefits are provided through insurance. In other words, if benefits are paid under an insurance contract issued by an insurance company (who collects premiums from the employer or employee), employees may be covered or excluded at the discretion of management. The insurance contract should, however, be reviewed to ensure that it properly identifies the excluded employee groups.

In contrast, "self-insured" medical and dental plans, which are plans underwritten by the employer and from which the employer pays claims, are subject to "non-discrimination rules" set forth in Section 105(h) of the Internal Revenue Code. These rules require some level of equalization of benefits among employees. If the plan does not comply with these rules, highly compensated employees may be taxed on the value of the excess benefits. Under these rules, the plan must:

- actually benefit at least 70% of all employees

  or

- actually benefit 80% of eligible employees if 70% or more of all employees are eligible for the plan

  or

- cover a class of employees that does not discriminate in favor of highly compensated employees. Acceptable classifications normally would include "all regular full-time employees," all employees of a given plant, division or subsidiary, or all non-bargaining unit employees. (Federal labor law requires that this exclusion be stated as follows: "The plan excludes all union-represented employees whose agreements were the subject of good-faith bargaining.") Classifications that include only executives, administrators, exempt employees or corporate headquarter employees will be suspect.

A self-insured plan may, without violating nondiscrimination rules:

- exclude employees with less than 3 years of service who are part-time, who have not reached age 25, who are covered by a union contract, or who are nonresident aliens with no income earned within the United States

- provide the same benefits to all participants. If all participants receive the same benefits, reimbursement must also be provided at the same level for all participants.

Note, however, that if an employer wants to provide excess benefits solely to highly compensated employees, it may do so simply by using an insurance company to insure the benefit.

Pension and profit sharing plans

The nondiscrimination rules applicable to tax qualified pension and profit sharing plans are complex. Section 410(b) of the Code provides minimum coverage and participation standards which, as a general rule of thumb, require either that:

- at least 70% of non-highly compensated employees actually benefit under the plan (the percentage test)

  or

- the percentage of non-highly compensated employees who benefit is at least 70% of the percentage of highly compensated employees who benefit under the plan (the ratio percentage test).

The plan may also pass this test by showing that the average benefit percentage (amount of benefits under all qualified retirement plans/compensation) of non-highly compensated employees is at least 70% of the average benefit percentage for highly compensated employees.

For example, assume that an employer with a benefit plan has 100 employees, and that:

- of the 100 employees, 30 are highly compensated employees (20 of which actually benefit under the plan)

- of the 100 employees, 70 are non-highly compensated employees (45 of which actually benefit under the plan).

The plan would not pass the percentage test because only 64% (45/70) of the non-highly compensated employees benefit under the plan.

The plan would pass the ratio percentage test because the percentage of non-highly compensated employees who benefit under the plan (64%, 45/70) is at least 70% of the percentage of highly compensated employees who benefit under the plan (66%, 20/30).

All non-union employees of all companies or divisions that are commonly owned within the same controlled group are considered together in applying these rules. A controlled group is a group of commonly owned companies that can be considered as one entity for federal tax purposes. Union employees are treated separately based upon their respective bargaining agreements. Employees of different companies or operations may also be considered separately if the entity employing them qualifies as a separate line of business.

An entity could qualify as a separate line of business and thus be considered separately from other commonly-owned companies or divisions for discrimination testing issues if all of the following requirements are met:

- It is a separate organizational unit.

- It has separate financial accountability.

- It has a separate employee work force.

- It has separate management.

- Each separate line of business has at least 50 employees.

Note that because the separate workforce and management requirements apply specific numerical tests, additional analysis is necessary to verify that these requirements are met. Such analysis is beyond the scope of this guide.

The IRS must also be notified in annual reports and in any determination letter request if separate lines of business are used to qualify the plan. Finally, the employer may not be permitted to utilize a standardized prototype plan if it relies upon separate lines of business for testing purposes.

The application of the non-discrimination tests to a newly acquired business can be delayed under a special merger and acquisition rule. Under this rule, employees of a newly acquired business are not required to be considered in coverage testing until the end of the first plan year following the plan year in which the acquisition occurred.

Finally, it is important to note that 401(k) deferred compensation plans are subject to additional discrimination rules. These rules limit the amount of compensation that highly compensated employees may defer to the plan, on a pre-tax basis, in proportion to amounts deferred by non-highly compensated employees. Similar rules limit the amount of matching contributions that an employer can make on behalf of highly compensated employees in proportion to the contributions that the employer can make on behalf of non-highly compensated employees.

Traditional anti-discrimination rules

Health benefit plans under the Americans with Disabilities Act (ADA)

The ADA makes it unlawful for an employer to discriminate on the basis of a disability against a qualified individual with a disability with regard to "fringe benefits available by virtue of employment." Medical benefit plans have always made distinctions in coverage based on health conditions. Thus, there is a tension between traditional underwriting techniques, which limit and identify risk on the basis of particular medical conditions and treatments, and the non-discrimination principles of the ADA.

Things an employer may do

- Offer insurance plans that comply with existing federal and state insurance laws regardless of any adverse impact on disabled individuals.

- Use a state-regulated carrier to provide coverage in accordance with accepted principles of risk assessment and/or risk classification, as required or permitted by state law, even if the result is limited coverage for disabled individuals.

- Maintain a self-insured plan that adheres to similar accepted principles of risk classifications even if the result is limited coverage for disabled individuals.

- Continue offering plans that limit coverage for procedures or treatments – for example, limiting the number of blood transfusions covered even though this would adversely effect hemophiliacs. However, treatments associated only with a particular disease may not be excluded (see page 145, **Things an employer may not do**).

- Continue offering plans that limit reimbursements for certain types of drugs or procedures, such as experimental drugs or procedures.

However, drugs or procedures associated only with a particular disease may not be excluded (see page 145, **Things an employer may not do**).

- Provide incentives such as lower deductibles or co-payments for employees who participate in wellness programs such as smoking cessation, weight loss, stress reduction or drug and alcohol programs.

- Continue offering plans that limit coverage on preexisting conditions, in accordance with the Health Insurance Portability and Accountability Act of 1996 (HIPAA).

Things an employer may not do

- Limit insurance for a disabled individual based on a particular disability. Thus, a plan may not exclude coverage for particular medical conditions such as AIDS, cancer or heart disease. A plan also may not exclude treatments or procedures that are associated only with a particular disease. For example, the plan could not prohibit payment for AZT, a drug used only to treat AIDS. Courts have also held that while a plan may exclude experimental treatment, it may not specifically exclude coverage for high dose chemotherapy with autologous bone marrow transplant (ABMT) because this treatment is associated only with cancer.

- Limit insurance for an individual based on other illegal reasons including health status, medical condition (physical and mental), claims experience under prior plans, receipt of health care, medical history, genetic information, or evidence of insurability.

- Enter into an insurance contract that would have the effect of discriminating against a disabled employee.

- Fire or refuse to hire an individual because of the employer's fear that such individual's condition might adversely impact future health plan costs.

- Fire or refuse to hire an individual because the individual or his or her family member or dependent has a disability not covered by the employer's current health insurance plan or that may increase the employer's future health care costs.

- Effective for the first plan year beginning after December 31, 1997, a medical benefit plan must provide coverage for mental and nervous disorders (excluding drug and alcohol treatment) on the same basis as other medical conditions unless doing so would increase premium cost by more than 1% per year.

Specifically, a plan that offers mental health benefits cannot impose an annual or lifetime cap on such benefits that differs from the cap imposed on major medical benefits. An employer may utilize other cost-control methods to limit amount, duration, and scope of mental health coverage, such as increased deductibles, co-payments, and out-of-pocket maximums. Other methods include limiting the number and frequency of visits, or requiring that participants meet physician referral requirements. It should be noted that courts have upheld long-term disability plans – as opposed to health plans – that cap mental health benefits at a different duration than other benefits.

HIPAA

For plan years beginning after June 30, 1997, HIPAA prevents group health plans from excluding coverage for preexisting conditions beyond 12 months. A preexisting condition is a health condition that existed (whether or not actually treated or diagnosed) in the six months before the individual was first eligible for plan coverage. The 12-month maximum exclusion period is reduced for each month that a new participant had prior health coverage (including individual coverage) and for waiting periods prior to eligibility. However, coverage before a 63 day break between jobs can be disregarded. In other words, a newly hired employee arriving from a job where he or she had coverage for at least 12 months would have no preexisting condition exclusion, as long as that earlier coverage had not been allowed to lapse for more than 63 days.

Plans may elect to apply a 12-month preexisting condition exclusion for categories of coverage that the prior plan did not include without regard to any period of prior coverage an employee may have had. For example, if the previous plan did not have prescription drug coverage, the new plan could exclude drug coverage for preexisting conditions for a full 12 months, regardless of an employee's prior coverage. The law includes procedures for determining whether and for how long an individual had prior coverage, and what the earlier plan did or did not cover. No preexisting condition exclusion can be applied to maternity coverage or to newborn or newly adopted children who are promptly enrolled in the plan. In the case of late enrollees (those who fail to enroll in the plan at the point they are first eligible to do so), plans can exclude coverage for preexisting conditions for up to 18 months. Plans must offer special enrollment opportunities for people whose need or eligibility for health coverage changes because of birth, death, marriage, divorce, etc., or because of a job loss that causes the individual to lose other coverage. The extended 18-month exclusionary period does not apply to these special enrollees.

Maternity benefits

Pregnancy, childbirth and related medical conditions must be treated in the same manner as any other health condition. Moreover, medical plans may not exclude benefits for childbirth for an employee or his spouse. However, plans are not required to provide maternity benefits to dependent children.

For plan years beginning after June 30, 1997, medical plans may not apply preexisting condition limitations to pregnancy and may not limit coverage for newborn or newly adopted children who are enrolled in the plan within 30 days of birth or adoption.

Effective for plan years beginning after January 1, 1997, medical plans must provide for at least a 48-hour hospital stay for a normal delivery and a 96-hour stay for a caesarean birth, unless the attending provider, after consultation with the mother, agrees to discharge the mother and her newborn earlier. (See also Chapter 9, **Sex discrimination**.)

Retirement plans and age discrimination

- With few exceptions, employees cannot be forced to retire at any given age. The ADEA does, however, contain an exception that allows forced retirement for someone who has been a bona fide executive or high-level policy maker for the 2-year period immediately before retirement and who is:

  - at least age 65

    and

  - entitled to an immediate, nonforfeitable annual retirement benefit of at least $44,000.

- Retirement plans may establish a "normal retirement age" (that is, a minimum age at which benefits become available or on which actuarially equivalent benefits are based).

- Employees must continue to accrue benefits after normal retirement age on the same basis as other employees.

- Benefit enhancements such as early retirement subsidies may be conditioned upon reaching a minimum age. Thus, for example, retirement incentives can be offered to workers who are age 55 or over. Maximum age limits, however, cannot be imposed; that is, an employer cannot offer enhancements only to employees between the ages of 55 and 65.

- Benefits may be coordinated with Medicare or Social Security. An employer may provide pension subsidies that supplement or "bridge" pension benefits until the employee becomes eligible for Social Security.

Chapter 18

Affirmative action

Federal contractors are prohibited from discriminating against applicants and employees because of their race, color, religion, national origin, gender, disability and Vietnam veteran or disabled veteran status, and are required to take affirmative action to ensure equal employment opportunities for all persons. These obligations apply to all contracting agencies of the government and to certain contractors and subcontractors who perform under government contracts.

Applicable laws

There are three sources under which federal contractor affirmative action obligations arise: Executive Order 11246, Section 503 of the Rehabilitation Act of 1973 and the Vietnam Era Veterans' Readjustment Assistance Act of 1974 (VEVRAA). These laws are administered and enforced by the Office of Federal Contract Compliance Programs (OFCCP).

Executive Order 11246

Executive Order 11246 (E.O. 11246) prohibits federal contractors from discriminating in employment because of race, color, religion, gender and national origin. E.O. 11246 also requires federal contractors to take affirmative action to ensure equal employment opportunity for persons in those protected categories.

Rehabilitation Act of 1973

Section 503 of the Rehabilitation Act of 1973 prohibits federal contractors and subcontractors from discriminating against employees or applicants because of their mental or physical disabilities and requires affirmative action to ensure equal employment opportunity for those persons.

An individual with a disability under Section 503 is a person who:

- has a physical or mental impairment which substantially limits one or more major life activities

    or

- has a record of such an impairment

    or

- is regarded as having such an impairment.

Vietnam Era Veterans' Readjustment Assistance Act of 1974 (VEVRAA)

VEVRAA protects qualified disabled veterans and veterans of the Vietnam era from discrimination in employment with federal contractors. It also requires federal contractors to take affirmative action to ensure equal employment opportunity for persons with protected-veteran status.

Disabled veterans are persons entitled to disability compensation by the Veterans' Administration for disability rated at 30% or more, or persons whose discharge or release from active duty was for a disability incurred or aggravated in the line of duty. Qualified disabled veterans are disabled veterans who are capable of performing jobs with reasonable accommodation for their disabilities.

Veterans of the Vietnam era are persons who served on active duty for more than 180 days, any part of which occurred between August 5, 1964 and May 7, 1975, and who were discharged with other than a dishonorable discharge. Veterans of the Vietnam era also include persons discharged or released from active duty for a service-connected disability if any part of the active duty was performed between August 5, 1964 and May 7, 1975.

Federal contractor defined

A federal contractor is a person, partnership or corporation doing business with the federal government. The definition of "federal contractor" includes prime contractors, which are contractors that hold a contract with the federal government, as well as subcontractors of a prime contractor or of one of the prime contractor's subcontractors. A subcontractor is a "federal contractor" if it has an arrangement to furnish supplies, services or the use of real or personal property necessary to the performance of any federal contract, or if it agrees to perform or assume any part of the obligation under a federal contract.

In addition, if one establishment within a company is a federal contractor, other establishments in the company will be deemed federal contractors if they are so closely connected to the contracting establishment that the establishments can be considered a "single entity." The following 5 factors are examined together in determining whether two or more establishments form a single entity:

1. common ownership

2. common directors and/or officers

3. de facto exercise of control

4. unified personnel policies emanating from a common source

5. dependency of operations.

Obligations of federal contractors

Affirmative action plans (AAPs)

Contractors or subcontractors are required to develop and maintain affirmative action plans if they have 50 or more employees and have contracts of $50,000 or more. In addition, contractors are required to have affirmative action plans covering employment of minorities and women if they have 50 or more employees and:

- have contracts which in any 12 month period total $50,000

  or

- serve as a depository of government funds in any amount

  or

- is a financial institution that is an issuing and paying agent for U.S. savings bonds and savings notes.

The OFCCP has issued regulations that govern the content of affirmative action plans. Under E.O. 11246, employers must develop and maintain a formal written affirmative action plan for each of its establishments. The plan must contain both a written portion and statistical analyses. The written portion of the plan includes provisions in which the employer reaffirms its equal employment policy, identifies problem areas and corrective actions in its personnel practices and policies, develops action-oriented programs, and assesses its achievement of the prior year's goals. The statistical analyses requires employers to divide the work force into job groups by skills or job content, wage rates and promotional opportunities. Employers then ascertain the availability of qualified, available women and minorities for each job group. The availability figures are compared to the employer's actual employment of women and minorities in each job group. Where women and minorities are under-utilized in comparison to their availability in the labor market, the employer must set goals and timetables to achieve full utilization of women and minorities in that job group.

Section 503 of the Rehabilitation Act and VEVRAA also require affirmative action plans. However, unlike E.O. 11246, the affirmative action plans for the disabled and protected veterans do not require statistical analyses. Rather, these Acts require a written plan that sets forth the contractor's efforts to recruit and hire qualified disabled persons and protected veterans. These affirmative action programs may be consolidated into one plan.

Affirmative action clause

Both the Rehabilitation Act and VEVRAA require federal contractors to include an affirmative action clause in contracts and subcontracts. Section 503 of the Rehabilitation Act requires that a six-paragraph affirmative action clause be included in all contracts and subcontracts of $10,000 or more. The clause is set forth at 41 C.F.R. § 60-741.4. The Act allows for the clause to be incorporated into contracts and subcontracts by reference.

VEVRAA requires prime and subcontractors to include a thirteen-paragraph affirmative action clause in all contracts and subcontracts of $10,000 or more. The clause is set forth at 41 C.F.R. § 60-250.4. VEVRAA also allows the clause to be incorporated in contracts and subcontracts by reference.

Equal opportunity clause

E.O. 11246, the Rehabilitation Act and VEVRAA require federal contractors to include an equal opportunity clause in contracts and subcontracts. The Rehabilitation Act and VEVRAA require the clause in federal contracts or subcontracts in excess of $10,000. E.O. 11246 requires the equal opportunity clause for:

- contracts or subcontracts with an aggregate total of $10,000 during any 12-month period

- contractors with government bills of lading

- depositories of federal funds in any amount

- financial institutions that are issuing and paying agents for U.S. savings bonds and savings notes.

The seven part equal opportunity clause required by E.O. 11246 is set forth at 41 C.F.R. § 60-1.4(a) and may be incorporated by reference in contracts and subcontracts. The clause provides that the contractor will not discriminate against any employee or applicant because of race, color, religion, sex, or national origin and will take affirmative action to ensure that applicants and employees are employed and treated during employment without regard to these characteristics.

Similarly, the equal opportunity clauses required by the Rehabilitation Act and VEVRAA prohibit discrimination based on disability and protected-veteran status, respectively, and require contractors to take affirmative action to ensure that employees and applicants are employed and treated during employment without regard to disability or protected-veteran status. The six paragraph equal opportunity clause under the Rehabilitation Act is set forth at 41 C.F.R. § 60-741.5, and its VEVRAA counterpart is contained in 41 C.F.R. § 60-250.4. These clauses may also be incorporated by reference.

Listing of job openings

In addition to prohibiting discrimination, VEVRAA requires federal contractors to list job openings with the local state employment service. The job openings to be listed include openings at the time of execution of the contract and openings that occur during the performance of the contract, whether or not generated by the contract. Openings for executives and top management, openings for 3 days or less and openings that will be filled from within the contractor's organization do not have to be listed.

Desegregation of facilities

Federal contractors to whom the E.O. 11246 equal opportunity clause requirement applies must also ensure that the facilities they provide for employees are not segregated on the basis of race, color, religion, gender, or national origin, except that facilities may be segregated to assure privacy between the sexes.

Enforcement

Executive Order 11246 is enforced by the Office of Federal Contract Compliance Programs (OFCCP) of the United States Department of Labor. The OFCCP's primary tools for monitoring compliance are an audit procedure known as a compliance review and the investigation of complaints. Audits and investigations may be conducted on- or off-site, or both, and are designed to supply information for a comprehensive analysis of the contractor's employment practices and policies regarding discrimination and affirmative action. The OFCCP first tries to resolve non-compliance informally, with an agreement by the contractor to correct deficiencies. The OFCCP may use administrative or court actions to enforce its regulations and orders if a settlement is not reached through informal discussions.

The OFCCP also is responsible for enforcing compliance by federal contractors with the requirements of the Rehabilitation Act of 1973 with respect to handicapped individuals and the Vietnam Era Veterans Readjustment Assistance Act of 1974 with respect to Vietnam veterans.

Penalties that may be imposed against contractors who violate these provisions include, among others:

- awarding back pay for affected applicants or employees

- terminating or suspending any contract

- publishing the name of the contractor as having failed to comply

- prohibiting the contractor from participation in government contracts for a fixed or indefinite term

- instituting criminal proceedings.

Chapter 19

Practical advice
for dealing with
employee discipline

Notwithstanding the extensive discussion of anti-discrimination laws in this guide, employers certainly may discipline employees for legitimate, performance-based reasons. However, employers should be prepared to show that the discipline was for a legitimate reason and not because of one of the prohibited bases discussed throughout this guide. By following the guidelines below, employers will reduce the risk of lawsuits and will be prepared to defend their decision.

An overview of the general legal concepts for handling problem employees

- The employer should implement and communicate its rules of conduct.

- The employer should communicate performance expectations.

- The employer must use candor in evaluating employee conduct.

- The employer must ensure uniform and consistent application of all standards and rules.

- Management should take prompt action on disciplinary and performance problems after conducting a thorough investigation.

- Management should attempt to remedy disciplinary and performance problems through progressive counseling and discipline whenever possible.

A problem employee is easiest to handle if the employer has well-established and effective personnel policies

- An employer should consider whether it needs an employee handbook or personnel policy which establishes disciplinary procedures.

    - The employer should retain discretion to address each situation on a case-by-case basis.

    - The handbook should have a disclaimer stating that it is not a contract. The disclaimer should be prominently displayed on the first page of the handbook.

    - The employer should periodically (at least once a year) review all written policies to make certain they are current and comply with applicable laws.

    - Employees should be required to sign a form acknowledging that they have received a copy of the handbook. The form should contain a disclaimer stating that the employee recognizes that the handbook is not a contract. These forms should be maintained in the employee's personnel file.

- The employer should have an established annual evaluation process.

    - The evaluation process ensures that both the employee and supervisor are aware of performance deficiencies.

    - The written evaluation serves as a specific record of performance, not only of the problem employee, but of others with whom the problem employee's performance could be compared.

    - The evaluation process forces management to establish legitimate performance goals.

    - The elements of an effective evaluation process include:

        - written evaluations, based on written criteria which are disseminated to all managers

        - evaluations that are conducted on a regularly scheduled basis

        - evaluations that include a forthright, honest appraisal of performance

- evaluations which avoid "grade inflation" (to a jury, "good" means good)

- evaluations which are reviewed by more than one level of management

- evaluations which are communicated to the employee

- evaluations which are not one-sided. The evaluation form should include a section for the employee to raise any objections or comments.

Disciplinary guidelines for handling problem employees

- Management should adhere to the timetable and procedures set forth in the handbook or disciplinary procedures.

  - Don't wait until a problem becomes serious. Supervisors should review employee performance on a regular basis.

  - When problems develop, the supervisor should discuss them with the employee and suggest ways of correcting the situation.

  - The supervisor should consider the employee's reasons for the behavior and explain why those are unacceptable. Such discussions should be documented and placed in the employee's file. Moreover, oral and written warnings should be given for specific problems.

  - A progressive discipline procedure of this kind should precede all future discipline except for extreme misconduct.

- If the undesirable behavior continues, the supervisor should involve higher management in the situation.

  - A meeting should be held between supervisors and the employee.

  - At the meeting the employee should be advised as to each action or activity which must be corrected. The employee must be cautioned that the failure to comply with the corrective action could result in termination.

- The final decision to terminate any employee **should not be made solely by the first-line supervisor**.

  - At least two levels of management should be involved in the decision.

- In difficult cases, an attorney should also be consulted before the decision is made.

- When contemplating the termination of an employee for gross misconduct (for example, theft, drug or alcohol use on premises, etc.) management should suspend the employee pending a final decision.

  - During the suspension period a thorough investigation of the situation should be made to assure that the employee's problems are both serious and thoroughly documented.

  - Prior to the final decision, the employee should be provided an opportunity to present his or her side directly to management.

  - Management should not discuss the investigation outside of a limited "need-to-know" group.

Termination checklist

- Is the rule or standard which the employee violated published?

- Did this employee ever receive a personal, written copy of the rule or standard (handbook)?

- Has management complied with the stated disciplinary guidelines? Unless the termination is for gross misconduct (which should not require a prior warning), has the employee received oral and written warnings?

- If other employees have violated this rule or order, did they receive the same disciplinary action as this employee?

- Does management have factual records on this and other employees covering all violations of this rule or order?

- Was the incident which triggered the final warning or discharge carefully investigated prior to taking serious or final disciplinary action?

- Does the investigative file include the identity of witnesses, dates, times, places and other pertinent factors on all past violations, including the most recent one?

- Does the degree of discipline imposed on this employee "fit" the:

  - seriousness of the proven offense?

  - the employee's past record?

  - the employee's length of service?

- Is the employee a member of a protected class?

Additional considerations for problem performers

- If the decision to terminate is based on poor performance, has the employee been given an opportunity to improve?

- Has the employee been specifically warned that if there is not sufficient improvement during a "probationary" period, he or she will be discharged?

- Has the employee been given an opportunity to meet with his or her supervisor during the probationary period?

- Has management been honest with the employee in all respects, including the possibility of termination?

- Is the employee a member of a protected class, and, if so, have others not in a protected class been terminated for the same reasons?

- Can the decision-makers articulate the reasons for termination succinctly, without hesitation, and without total reliance on subjective comments such as "he/she just didn't have it?"

Formalizing the employment termination decision

- Management should have a third party (for example, someone from the human resources department) review the facts and participate in the decision.

  - Third party review makes the decision appear fair and well-reasoned.

  - If the same "third party" is used for all cases, that person can help to assure uniform application of performance standards, disciplinary policy, and level of punishment.

- Management should review the decision from a jury's perspective. For example, regardless of established policy, does the decision seem fair? Does the punishment fit the offense?

- Management should weigh the cost of potential litigation (time, money, and potential effect on other employees) against the benefits derived from termination of the employee.

Communicating the termination decision

- Management should communicate the decision in person.

  - More than one supervisor should be present for the termination meeting.

  - Decide in advance who will say what and rehearse delivery.

  - Designate one individual as a note-taker. That person should record everyone's comments.

  - The reason(s) given for the termination should be the true reason(s).

    - Be sure to communicate all the reasons for termination.

    - If there are several reasons for termination and each represents an independent and sufficient basis for termination, then make that clear.

    - Allow the employee to examine supporting documentation, if appropriate.

  - The reason(s) given should be as direct and as specific as the circumstances warrant.

    - Resist a natural reluctance to reveal misgivings about employee's intelligence, honesty, etc. Lack of candor here will reflect badly on the employer during trial, if the employee sues.

    - While it is not necessary to reveal every detail of the decision-making process, the employee should be given at least enough of an explanation to ensure that he/she understands:

      - The reasons being relied upon by the employer

      - The fact that the decision was made by more than one individual

      - That the employer followed established procedure in making the decision.

- Choose the least inflammatory language. For example, describe the issue as one of "trust" instead of labeling an employee a thief; describe an employee's performance as inadequate instead of labeling him/her incompetent.

- Allow the employee another opportunity to tell his/her side of the story.

  - This reduces the likelihood that the "story" will change after termination.

  - This reduces the likelihood that the employee will sue just to have an opportunity to be heard.

  - This may alert the personnel department to any potential problems before the termination becomes effective.

- Be prepared to respond to questions or indicate a willingness to reply.

- Management should be conscious of the employee's discomfort and embarrassment. A humiliated employee is a likely candidate for litigation.

  - Conduct the meeting at the end of the work day.

  - Give the employee time to regain his or her composure.

  - Do not have the employee "escorted" off the premises with a box of personal belongings during the middle of the work day.

- Management should beware of high risk situations.

  - If a "red flag" is spotted, then particular care must be given to the review process.

  - Examples of red flag situations include:

    - Decision-maker's anger.

    - On-the-spot terminations.

    - Decision by new or inexperienced supervisor.

    - Long-term employee.

    - Employee within a protected group is to be replaced by an individual outside the protected group.

- Management should make certain that the terminated employee receives all benefits for which he/she is eligible: vested vacation pay, COBRA, etc.

  - With a long-term employee who may need to make important benefits decisions, consider setting up a time for the employee to meet with the employer's employee benefits personnel to discuss such matters. Give the employee time to accept the termination decision before requiring him or her to make such decisions.

  - Provide the employee with all notices for continued benefit coverage to which he or she is entitled under COBRA.

Post-discharge issues

- References.

  - A policy of neutral references (verifying dates of employment and positions held) is generally the best course. All inquiries should be directed to the personnel or human resources department.

  - Unfavorable references may form the basis for a lawsuit under defamation and/or other legal theories. While there may be a qualified privilege and truth is a defense, these claims are so fact-specific, they often have to be litigated.

- Contesting unemployment compensation.

  - In most states, a discharged employee may collect unemployment benefits unless the employer establishes that the employee was discharged for "misconduct connected with work." Therefore, a discharge for poor performance will ordinarily not disqualify an individual from receiving unemployment compensation.

  - If a discharged employee has already filed a charge, claim or lawsuit, the employer may be wise not to appeal a questionable unemployment claim to the hearing level because this will enable the former employee to engage in "free" discovery.

- Requests for personnel file.

  - In most states, an employee (or an individual terminated within a specific period of time prior to making the request) may make a request to inspect and copy his/her personnel file. This is often a warning that litigation will follow.

- While there are certain materials that may be withheld, if materials required to be produced are withheld, there are certain penalties associated with non-disclosure.

- Make sure the personnel file actually includes all personnel material. Conversely, simply because materials may be in a file does not render them disclosable. If uncertain whether certain materials must be disclosed, an attorney should be consulted.

Chapter 20

Management of discrimination charges

The first step employees or applicants must take when suing an employer for illegal discrimination is to file a charge of discrimination. Depending on what type of discrimination is claimed, the charge may be filed with the EEOC, a comparable state fair employment agency, the OFCCP, the NLRB or OSHA. The experience of reviewing a charge of discrimination often will produce immediate reaction rather than reason; the recipient may wish to treat the charge with outrage and disbelief. Unfortunately, these emotions may compromise the opportunity for favorable resolution of the charge. In most cases, an orderly, stepwise analysis of the **facts** will produce a swift and satisfactory result. The key approach should be one of careful and thoughtful analysis of the facts followed by an effective and easy-to-understand presentation of the facts in the light most favorable to the employer.

1. **First step**
   Schedule a time when a careful analysis of the charge can be conducted. In most cases, there will be ample time to gain a full understanding of what is being charged (and, equally important, what is not being charged). Take the time available; the consequences of a loss due to inadequate investigation or analysis can be financially severe.

   Note
   If there is any doubt about what is being alleged as a factual matter, contact the agency and ask for immediate clarification. **Do not act on wrong assumptions about what is being claimed by the charging party. Do not guess about what the employer is being charged with.**

2. **Second step**
   Make a written list of the facts that pertain to the charge. The list should include:

   - the allegations made by the charge

   - a statement-by-statement assessment of the truth of each allegation (after there has been an opportunity to determine the truth of the statements)

   - the name and work history of the complaining employee or ex-employee

   - the names and locations of the individual's immediate supervisors and (if different) those who evaluated the individual's performance

- the names and locations of those who made the decisions on which the charge appears to be based

- the names and locations of those who will likely be regarded as "comparables" (those employees or former employees outside a protected class whose performance or circumstances of employment are similar to those of the charging party) by the agency investigator (and by the charging party's lawyers in case the matter proceeds to formal hearing).

Make a time-line of the events related to the charge and your response.

3. **Third step**
   Prepare a draft response to the charge. Include in the response some background information about the employer's business and the charging party's role or former role in that business. Include personnel information such as the date of hire and jobs held prior to the action that is being challenged by the charge.

   Note
   The object is to convey to the investigator a frame of reference in which to assess the merits of the charge; it is not desirable to allow the investigator to proceed only with the frame of reference provided by the charging party. Do not finalize the response until it has been reviewed by at least one other person who is knowledgeable of the facts.

   Remember

   - The initial response to the charge may be used in future proceedings related to the charge, and in whatever agency or court the case may wind up being considered. Any later change may be regarded as evidence that the response was false and was falsified to cover up illegal activity. **Do not make any response to the charge until you are satisfied that you know all of the facts that pertain to the charge and that the position stated in the response is the correct position.** You should also include language in your response indicating that the position statement is not intended as an affidavit and is based upon your understanding of the facts at this stage of the proceeding, thereby reserving the opportunity to modify or add to the response.

   - The existence of **factual** disputes between what the charging party has represented to the agency and what the employer represents to the agency may cause the case to be referred for hearing regardless of how the agency investigator feels about the case. The agency investigator has a great many other cases to be addressed. Make it as easy as possible for the investigator to understand your case and to conclude that the charge is unfounded. **Avoid making an issue of facts that are not actually in dispute or not related to the charging party's claims.**

- The charging party has the right to file a charge even if the charge is wrong. The penalties for retaliation based on the filing of a charge can be as severe as the penalties for discrimination based on race, color, age, gender or other protected factors. Agencies aggressively guard their processes. **Avoid criticisms of the charging party's filing of the charge.**

- Protesting "too much" can lead to the impression that the protester actually is hiding something. Be objective and restrained. Avoid exaggerated denials of the allegations. Do not boast of the employer's record of diversity or EEO record, if not directly related to the allegations.

Documents

Most charges of discrimination raise questions about the contents of documents. These include, for example:

- employment policies

- work rules

- handbooks

- promotion tests

- personnel files

- written personnel evaluations

- job descriptions.

Make certain that your response to the charge is consistent with such documents, and, if not, take the time to fully understand the reasons for any inconsistencies. Many employers have found themselves in uncomfortable positions when confronted with such inconsistencies **after** having submitted a statement of position.

Comparables

Most charges are based on **inferences** that protected characteristics motivated the action taken. Very few charges are based on actual direct evidence or admissions of illegal conduct. The primary inference of illegal discrimination is the comparison of the treatment the charging party received with that of another employee who is of a different race, gender, age or other protected factor. For example, an employee terminated during a reduction in force may claim that she was selected for termination because of her gender, claiming she had the same qualifications and performance as male employees who remained employed. To prevail against such a charge, the employer must show a reason other than gender, such as her having the least seniority, to explain why the female employee was selected for termination.

If the charge fails to list any comparables, or omits some obvious comparables, the failure and omission may be deliberate. Pointing this out may be helpful as a part of the response.

Media questions

There is usually no reason or justification for responding to media questions during the investigation stage.

Practical tip: don't respond.

Internal questions

There is usually no reason or justification for responding to internal questions during the investigation stage.

Practical tip: don't respond. **Maintain your investigation on a *strict* need-to-know basis**.

Lawyers

There are 3 points to remember:

1. Seeking advice of a lawyer regarding the initial response to the charge will be more efficient than seeking advice on how to undo the effects of a bad response (the "pay me now or pay me later" theory).

2. Plaintiff's lawyers may be contacting you with "questions." Your answers may be used against the employer at a later date. **You have no legal obligation to deal with or even respond to lawyers for the charging party at this stage.**

3. The attorney-client privilege will be lost to the extent that you discuss the employer's case with anyone who is not within the need-to-know group. If you elect to work with a lawyer for the employer at this stage, ask the lawyer for advice on how to handle drafts of the response, other documents and witness statements so that the privilege may be maintained.

Witness statements

"Statements" include not only sworn and signed affidavits, but also include notes made during interviews, recollections of oral conversations, diary and log entries. Most discrimination laws provide means for the investigating officer or the charging party's attorney to obtain statements given to or in the possession of the employer at some point.

Destruction of statements after a charge has been filed may have severe consequences. Therefore, the employer should maintain copies of the statements and any other relevant documents. In the event a statement appears to include information adverse to the employer, a response should be prepared so that the adverse information can be explained.

Departing witnesses

Agency investigations are not promptly concluded in most cases. This is a product of caseload rather than complexity. It is not uncommon for witnesses to change location, to be terminated, or to resign during the investigation process. Be aware of this possibility and make certain that you are made aware of such an occurrence as soon as possible. When a witness leaves the employ of the employer, the employer may need to take steps to preserve the witness' information. If this issue arises, you may want to consult an attorney.

Chapter 21

Discrimination prohibited by state law

State laws prohibit discrimination because of personal characteristics (for example, race, gender, age, disability) covered by Title VII, the ADEA and the ADA. In addition, many states prohibit discrimination based on factors not covered by federal law, including marital status, arrest and conviction records, lawful use of products outside the workplace, political activities, the exercise of civil rights such as voting or serving on a jury, whistleblowing, filing workers' compensation claims and seeking access to personnel records. Factors or conduct protected from discrimination vary from state to state. This chapter provides an overview of the characteristics most frequently protected by state laws.

Marital status

Twenty-seven states prohibit marital status discrimination. A chart showing which states protect employees against marital status discrimination is set forth on pages 178-179. Claims based on marital status discrimination are usually filed with the appropriate state civil rights agency and investigated much like a discrimination charge filed with the Equal Employment Opportunity Commission.

The critical question that arises under state marital status discrimination laws is whether the term "marital status" means only the legal status of being married, single, divorced, separated or widowed or also includes the identity of one's spouse. Spousal identity refers to the particular person an individual is married to, not whether an individual is married. For example, an employer may refuse to promote an employee if the result would be that the employee would be supervised by his spouse. Whether this constitutes marital status discrimination depends on the state law. If marital status is defined only as the legal status of being married, the refusal to promote the employee would not be discrimination. If, on the other hand, the state law prohibits discrimination based on the identity of the spouse, then the failure to promote the employee would be unlawful.

Other examples of spousal identity issues include situations where an employee's spouse works for a competitor and the employer fears that the employee is disclosing confidential information to the spouse or where one spouse is terminated for misconduct and the employer fears a morale problem if the other spouse is allowed to remain employed. If the state defines marital status to include the identity of the spouse, then terminating employees in these situations could violate state law.

Anti-nepotism policies

The highest courts in some states, including Illinois, Michigan and New York, have concluded that marital status discrimination does not extend to spousal identity, but is based solely on an individual's legal status of being married, single, divorced, separated or widowed. The highest state courts in other states, including Hawaii, Montana and Minnesota, have held that spousal identity is included within the definition of marital status. However, even where a state interprets marital status discrimination as including spousal identity, an employer's anti-nepotism rule may be upheld on the basis of business necessity. The business necessity defense may be proven by showing that the application of an anti-nepotism policy against a spouse is necessary to ensure efficient job performance.

Arrest and conviction records

Individual states often regulate the use of criminal history information. The extent to which this information may be used varies from state to state.

More than half of the states have enacted legislation restricting an employer's consideration of a person's criminal history record. A chart showing which states regulate an employer's use of a person's criminal past is set forth on pages 180-187. From this chart, the following generalizations can be made regarding those states that limit the use of criminal record information:

- discrimination based on an arrest record is usually prohibited

- discrimination based on criminal records that have been deleted or sealed is usually prohibited

- employers may consider an individual's criminal conviction if the conviction relates to the position sought.

Employers should be aware that many states require criminal background checks of applicants for certain occupations, usually where employees come into contact with children. For example, Illinois law requires all prospective teachers and educational support personnel to submit to a criminal background investigation and the applicant cannot be hired if the investigation reveals that he or she was convicted of certain crimes.

Even if state law allows employers to rely on arrest and conviction records in making employment decisions, employers should know that Title VII may limit employers' use of the records. Through the application of Title VII of the Civil Rights Act of 1964, minorities have long been protected from discrimination based on having a criminal record. An employment practice that rejects applicants solely because of an arrest or conviction record has been found to have an adverse impact against minorities, even if it is evenly applied among all applicants regardless of their race. The adverse impact stems from the fact that minorities are involved with the criminal justice system substantially more frequently than non-minorities in proportion to their representation in the population. Consequently, a practice that denies employment to persons because of their criminal records will be declared unlawful unless it is justified by a showing of business necessity.

The EEOC has issued a policy guidance on the consideration of arrest and conviction records in employment decisions. The EEOC views arrest and conviction records differently.

Arrest records

The EEOC considers it unlawful to have a blanket prohibition on employing persons with arrest records. Arrest records are not considered to be reliable evidence of whether an individual committed a criminal act. Therefore, the EEOC requires employers to examine the circumstances surrounding the arrest by, among other things, offering the applicant an opportunity to explain his or her arrest record. If, after its investigation, the employer reasonably concludes that the applicant engaged in the conduct for which he or she was arrested, the conduct occurred recently, and the conduct is job-related, the employer may exclude the applicant from consideration. Under these circumstances, the EEOC permits the employer to consider the conduct, not the fact of an arrest, in assessing the suitability of the applicant for the position sought.

Conviction records

In contrast to arrest records, the EEOC has stated that a conviction record may be relied upon as conclusive evidence that the person committed a crime. Nevertheless, conviction records may not be used as an absolute prohibition to employment. Therefore, the EEOC has stated that any decision to reject an applicant due to his or her criminal convictions should be based on 3 considerations:

1. the nature and seriousness of the offense(s) for which the person was convicted

2. the amount of time that has passed since the person was convicted and/or completed his sentence

3. the job-relatedness of the conviction.

Discrimination against smokers and lawful use of products statutes

Increasingly, employers have limited smoking in the workplace, sometimes by limiting it to designated areas and sometimes by prohibiting it outright. At the same time, the gap between the insurance costs of smokers and non-smokers has grown. Thus, employers have faced growing incentives to discriminate against smokers in the workplace.

In response, over half the states have enacted laws that protect smokers against workplace discrimination. These laws fall into two general categories. First, "smokers' rights" statutes deal specifically with the use of tobacco and explicitly protect smokers from workplace discrimination. Similarly, "lawful use of products" statutes prohibit discrimination based on the lawful use of products, such as tobacco, outside the workplace. Although laws in the second category are frequently understood to be "smoking laws," they may well have broader application (for instance, to the use of alcohol). The chart on pages 178-179 lists those states that currently have smokers' rights laws or lawful use of products statutes.

Typically, smokers' rights and lawful use of products laws still allow employers to treat smokers and non-smokers differently in providing insurance. Thus, while under such laws an employer cannot refuse to hire or otherwise discriminate against an employee solely because that employee smokes, the employer may still provide health insurance under which employees who smoke are charged higher premiums than those who do not.

Public employees may have different rights with respect to smoking than private employees. For instance, Arizona and Tennessee both have smokers' rights statutes that apply only to public employees. In addition, in an Oklahoma case, a federal appellate court struck down a one-year smoking ban for firefighter trainees, finding that the ban was not related to on-the-job performance and thus infringed upon the applicants' constitutional rights as public employees.

Political activities

Almost every state prohibits employers from discriminating against employees because of their political activities. However, these laws vary greatly in scope. In some states the prohibition is very broad. For instance, California employers may not adopt or enforce rules or policies that prevent their employees from engaging or participating in politics or from becoming candidates for political office. Other states have more specific prohibitions. In Minnesota, for example, employees who give proper notice and who are members of central or executive committees of political parties may take paid absences for party meetings, and employees who are selected as election judges may take unpaid leaves.

Conversely, many states have laws that prohibit employers from discriminating against employees for **refusing** to engage in certain political activities. For instance, New Mexico's law provides that an employer cannot punish an employee if the employee refuses to make political contributions.

Voting

Most states also have laws protecting employees from discrimination resulting from the exercise of their right to vote. Some statutes provide that employers must permit employees a certain number of hours of leave in order to vote, such as Wisconsin (3 hours) and Georgia (2 hours). Other states' requirements are less specific. Under North Dakota's law, for example, employers are "encouraged" to establish rules allowing employees voting absences when necessary. Many state laws also specifically prohibit employers from threatening or coercing employees to vote in a particular manner.

Jury duty

State laws frequently prohibit discrimination against employees who are called to serve on juries. Under some state laws, an employee who is fired for serving on a jury may sue the employer for back pay and reinstatement. In addition, an employer who stands in the way of an employee called to serve on a jury may be held in contempt of court.

Volunteer firefighting and emergency services

A few states have laws that prohibit employers from discriminating against employees who serve as volunteer firefighters or emergency personnel. For instance, in Indiana, a volunteer firefighter who is absent from work because of emergency firefighting activity or who leaves work for such activity with a supervisor's permission may not be disciplined for his or her absence. Other states confine this prohibition to government employees.

Employment tests

Although various forms of employee testing have become a common part of the employment landscape, state law often prohibits the discriminatory use of certain forms of testing.

Lie detector tests

The use of lie detector tests by employers is highly controversial, and in most states an employer cannot discriminate against an employee who fails to take a lie detector test. In many states, such as New York, lie detector tests by employers are prohibited outright. In other states, such as Pennsylvania, lie detector tests are permitted only if the employee is informed that the test is voluntary, and the employer does not make taking the test a condition of hiring or continued employment.

Genetic tests

The use of genetic testing in employment is an area addressed by few states. Rhode Island, for example, has a law that prohibits an employer from requesting or administering a genetic test as a condition of employment. Employers should be aware that this is an area that may produce new legislation and court rulings in additional states in the future.

Drug and alcohol testing

Almost half the states place some limits, either by statute or case law, on an employer's ability to subject employees or job applicants to drug and alcohol tests. For instance, such laws may limit the types of jobs for which testing may be required, require a certain level of suspicion or probable cause prior to testing, or require certain testing procedures.

Retaliation

The laws of many states also prohibit employers from taking action against employees who take certain legal or administrative actions.

Whistleblowing

Whistleblower protection laws generally prohibit employers from taking adverse actions against employees who in good faith report suspected violations of law to public authorities. Some whistleblower laws, such as Alaska's, apply specifically to public employees. Others, like North Dakota's, apply to all employees. Moreover, in some states that do not have whistleblower statutes, courts have found employers liable for taking action against whistleblowers on other grounds, such as public policy.

Workers' compensation

State laws frequently protect employees who file workers' compensation claims from retaliation. Such laws often provide that employers who take action against employees for pursuing workers' compensation claims may be sued for back pay, reinstatement and attorneys' fees. In addition, such laws may prohibit employers from asking prospective employees about previous workers' compensation claims. State anti-retaliation laws may also provide that employees who participate in a workers' compensation proceeding are protected from retaliation.

Personnel records

Most states have laws that allow employees the right to inspect, review, copy or make additions to their personnel records. At least one state, Illinois, provides that an employer who takes action against an employee for pursuing his or her rights under that state's personnel records review law may be sued by the employee and may also be criminally liable for the adverse action.

Non-work related activities

A few states, such as Colorado, New York, and North Dakota, have statutes that prohibit an employer from discriminating against employees on the basis of lawful activities outside of work hours. New York's law, for example, prohibits discrimination on the basis of an employee's "legal recreational activities outside of work hours" as long as those activities are "off the premises and without use of the employer's equipment or other property." The potential scope of such laws is extremely broad. For instance, one New York court has held that an employee who claimed she was demoted because she cohabited with another employee who had been discharged could sue her employer under New York's "legal recreational activities" law.

State laws prohibiting marital discrimination			**State laws regulating smoking**		
	YES	NO	Smokers rights statute	Lawful use of products statute	No statute at all
Alabama		x			x
Alaska	x				x
Arizona		x	X (public employees only)		
Arkansas		x			x
California	x				x
Colorado	x*			x	
Connecticut	x		x		
Delaware	x				x
Dist of Columbia	x		x		
Florida	x				x
Georgia		x			x
Hawaii	x				x
Idaho		x			x
Illinois	x			x	
Indiana		x	x		
Iowa	x**				x
Kansas	x***				x
Kentucky		x	x		
Louisiana		x	x		
Maine	x**		x		
Maryland	x				x
Massachusetts	x**				x
Michigan	x				x
Minnesota	x			x	
Mississippi		x	x		
Missouri		x	X (smoking, alcohol only)		
Montana	x			x	
Nebraska	x				x

	YES	NO	Smokers rights statute	Lawful use of products statute	No statute at all
Nevada		X		X	
New Hampshire	X		X		
New Jersey	X		X		
New Mexico		X	X		
New York	X			X	
North Carolina		X		X	
North Dakota	X			X	
Ohio	X				X
Oklahoma		X	X		
Oregon	X		X		
Pennsylvania		X			X
Rhode Island		X	X		
South Carolina		X	X		
South Dakota		X	X		
Tennessee		X	X		
Texas		X			X
Utah		X			X
Vermont		X			X
Virginia	X		X (public employees only)		
Washington	X				X
West Virginia		X	X		
Wisconsin	X			X	
Wyoming		X	X		

*   Colorado law makes it unlawful to terminate an employee or fail to hire a person "solely on the basis that such employee or person is married to or plans to marry another employee of the employer."

**   Marital status discrimination applies only to certain public sector employers.

***   Kansas law prohibiting gender discrimination has been interpreted to forbid employers from treating married women differently than married men and from denying women employment based on anti-nepotism policies.

State restrictions on the ability of employers to inquire or consider arrest and conviction records

State	Arrest	Conviction
AL	No	No
AK	No	No
AZ	No	Unless the conviction bears a reasonable relationship to job functions, public employees cannot be disqualified from employment solely because of a prior conviction. This provision is not applicable to law enforcement agencies.
AR	No	No
CA	Employers are prohibited from inquiring into or utilizing in determining any condition of employment information concerning an arrest. Arrests for which the employee is released on bail or on his or her own personal recognizance pending trial are excluded. Peace officers and certain health care workers are excluded from the protection of this statute.	No
CO	Employers cannot require an applicant to disclose any information contained in a sealed arrest record for which: (1) the person was not charged; (2) the charges were dismissed; or (3) the person was acquitted.	No

State	Arrest	Conviction
CT	Public employers cannot use arrest records that have not resulted in a conviction in connection with an application for employment. In the private sector, only personnel department employees and the person in charge of employment may have access to the portion of a job application form that contains information on a job applicant's arrest record.	Public employers cannot disqualify a person from employment solely because of a prior criminal conviction or consider conviction records that have been expunged. If an employer uses a conviction as the basis for rejecting an applicant, the applicant must be so notified in writing.
D.C.	No	No
DE	Employers may inquire about arrests, however, an offense that has been expunged does not have to be disclosed as an arrest.	No
FL	No	Except for certain drug, felony or first degree misdemeanor convictions directly related to the position applied for, public employers cannot disqualify a person from employment solely because of a prior criminal conviction. This provision is not applicable to firefighter applicants or applicants for employment with law enforcement or correctional agencies.
GA	The Georgia Crime Information Center is authorized to send criminal history records to employers, except it may not provide records of arrests, charges, and sentences for crimes relating to first offenders who have been discharged without a guilty finding.	By law, persons discharged without a guilty finding are not considered convicted of a crime and a discharge cannot be used by employers as a basis upon which to disqualify a job applicant. The Georgia Crime Information Center is authorized to send criminal history records to employers. Should an employer make an adverse decision regarding a person whose record was requested, the employer must notify the person that it obtained his criminal record, the contents of his record, and the effect the record had upon its decision.

State	Arrest	Conviction
HI	Employers are prohibited from discriminating against individuals because of an "arrest or court record." The definition of an "arrest or court record" includes any information about an individual's arrest.	The definition of "arrest or court record" also includes any information about a conviction by a law enforcement or military authority. Therefore, employers are prohibited from discriminating against individuals on the basis of prior criminal convictions. This prohibition does not extend to school or financial institutions in certain circumstances.
ID	No	No
IL	Employers cannot inquire into or use in connection with a term or condition of employment the fact of an arrest that was ordered expunged, sealed or impounded. The prohibition does not extend to obtaining or using "other information which indicates that a person actually engaged in the conduct for which he or she was arrested."	No
IN	No	No
IA	No	No
KS	Subject to disclosures, an applicant may state he was never arrested if his arrest record was expunged.	Subject to certain exceptions, an applicant may state he was never convicted if his conviction record was expunged.
KY	No	Except for specific crimes and crimes that directly relate to the position sought, no person can be disqualified from public employment because of a prior criminal conviction.

State	Arrest	Conviction
LA	No	A person shall not be disqualified or held ineligible to practice in any trade, occupation or profession for which a license, permit or certificate is required by the state solely because of a prior criminal record. A decision on eligibility must be in writing and explicitly state the reasons.
ME	No	No
MD	Employers are prohibited from: (1) requiring applicants to disclose information concerning criminal charges that have been expunged; and (2) refusing to hire or discharging a person solely because of his or her refusal to disclose information related to criminal charges that have been expunged.	No
MA	Employers are prohibited from inquiring into, or using in connection with a person's employment, an arrest that did not result in a conviction.	Except in limited circumstances, employers are prohibited from inquiring into, or using in connection with a person's employment, a: (1) first conviction for certain misdemeanors; or (2) misdemeanor conviction after a certain length of time.
MI	Except for pending felony charges, employers are prohibited from requesting information regarding an arrest that did not result in a conviction. This prohibition does not extend to law enforcement agencies.	No

State	Arrest	Conviction
MN	Public employers are prohibited from using in connection with an application for employment arrest records not followed by a valid conviction.	No person may be disqualified from public employment nor shall any person be disqualified from any occupation for which a license is required solely on the basis of a prior conviction unless the crime relates directly to the position of employment.
MO	No	No
MS	No	No
MT	No	No
NE	No	No
NV	Employers may inquire about arrests. However, if the applicant's arrest record is sealed, that applicant can state that he or she has no arrest record.	Employers may inquire about convictions. However, if the applicant's conviction or indictment records are sealed, the applicant can state that he or she has no convictions or indictments.
NH	State employee applicants do not have to answer questions about arrests or indictments.	No
NJ	Civil service applicants for law enforcement, firefighter and correctional officer positions may be questioned as to any arrest. An arrest or conviction that has been expunged is deemed not to have occurred.	Applicants for civil service positions may be questioned as to their criminal convictions and may be declared ineligible if the applicant was convicted of a crime which adversely relates to the employment sought. Except for law enforcement, firefighter or correctional officer positions, an appointing authority cannot reject an applicant based on criminal convictions that have been pardoned or expunged.

State	Arrest	Conviction
NM	An arrest record not followed by a valid conviction shall not be used in connection with an application for public employment.	Applicants and employees of the state may be denied employment if convicted of a felony or misdemeanor involving moral turpitude and the criminal conviction directly relates to the employment. The employer must state in writing the reasons for the decision. Conviction shall not operate as an automatic bar from obtaining public employment.
NY	Unless specifically allowed by law and except for police or peace officer applicants, it is unlawful to inquire into, or to act upon adversely, any: (1) arrest; or (2) criminal accusation that was followed by the termination of the criminal action in favor of the accused.	Employers are prohibited from discriminating against job applicants who have been previously convicted of one or more crimes unless: (1) there is a direct relationship between the crime and the job applied for; or (2) granting employment would involve an unreasonable risk to property or to the safety of individuals.
NC	No	No
ND	No	No
OH	An applicant cannot be questioned with respect to any arrest where the records have been expunged.	Employers are prohibited from inquiring into a job applicant's convictions that have been sealed, unless the question bears a direct and substantial relationship to the position.
OK	Employers are prohibited from requiring job applicants to disclose arrest records that have been sealed.	Employers are prohibited from requiring job applicants to disclose convictions that have been sealed.

State	Arrest	Conviction
OR	Employers may request arrest records less than one year old on which there has been no acquittal or dismissal from the state police, provided notice is given to the individual about whom the request is made. Employers are prohibited from discriminating against persons because of arrests that may be part of a juvenile record that has been expunged.	Employers may request conviction records from the state police, provided notice is given to the individual about whom the request is made. Employers are prohibited from discriminating against persons because of convictions that may be part of a juvenile record.
PA	No	Employers may consider the felony and misdemeanor convictions of job applicants if: (1) the convictions relate to the applicant's suitability for employment and (2) the applicant is informed in writing that the employer's decision not to hire the applicant was based in whole or in part on the applicant's criminal history record.
RI	Except for law enforcement or related positions, employers cannot ask a job applicant whether he or she was ever arrested or charged with any crime.	Employers may inquire into whether an applicant was ever convicted of a crime. A person whose conviction has been expunged may answer that he or she has never been convicted.
SC	No	No
SD	No	No
TN	No	No
TX	No	No
UT	A person who has received expungement and sealing of an arrest record may answer an inquiring employer as though the arrest did not occur.	Except for certain felonies, a person whose conviction has been expunged may answer an inquiring employer as though the conviction did not occur.

State	Arrest	Conviction
VT	No	No
VA	Employers are prohibited from requiring job applicants to disclose information concerning any arrest that has been expunged.	No
WA	Except for law enforcement agencies, it is an unfair practice for an employer to refuse to hire or otherwise discriminate against a person because he or she was arrested.	Except for law enforcement agencies, it is an unfair practice to refuse to hire or otherwise discriminate against a person simply because he or she was convicted of a crime. However, convictions may be considered if they relate to specific qualifications for the job and: (1) all applicants are treated alike; and (2) the conviction or the individual's release from prison, whichever is more recent, occurred less than 7 years ago.
WV	No	No
WI	Except for arrest records on pending charges or when employment depends on the bondability of the individual, employers are prohibited from requesting arrest record information or otherwise discriminating against an individual because of his arrest record.	Except for: (1) burglar alarm installers, (2) convictions that substantially relate to the circumstances of the particular job, or (3) when employment depends on the bondability of the individual, employers are prohibited from discriminating against an individual because of his or her conviction record.
WY	No	No

Practical pointers

An employer **MAY**:

Marital status

- Prohibit a husband and wife from working together, provided the applicable state law does not define "marital status" as the identity of one's spouse.

- Charge higher employee contributions for family insurance.

- Ask an applicant if he/she can meet specific work hours or schedules.

Arrest and conviction records

- Ask applicants whether they were ever convicted of a felony, so long as applicants are informed that a conviction record will not completely rule out employment.

- Ask an applicant about the surrounding circumstances of a criminal conviction if the conviction relates to the position sought.

- Discipline an employee who lied on his employment application regarding whether he was previously convicted of a crime (if the conviction was not sealed or expunged).

Practical pointers

An employer **MAY NOT**:

Marital status

• Ask applicants whether they are married.

• Provide single salespersons more lucrative out-of-town sales opportunities on the assumption that married employees could not meet travel requirements.

• Demote an employee because he or she became divorced.

Arrest and conviction records

• Refuse to hire an applicant based solely on an arrest record.

• Refuse to hire an applicant because of a criminal record that has been deleted.

• Maintain a blanket policy of prohibiting the employment of any applicant who was previously convicted of any crime.

Chapter 22

Discrimination based on credit history

Title VII of the Civil Rights Act prohibits discrimination against individuals on the basis of race, color, religion, sex or national origin. Most employers recognize that different treatment of individuals because of one or more of these five impermissible bases constitutes unlawful discrimination. However, unlawful discrimination also occurs when an employer maintains policies or practices that appear to be neutral, but have an adverse effect (disparate impact) on members of one or more of these protected classes that cannot be justified by business necessity.

This chapter addresses two situations in which disparate impact discrimination may occur. The first situation involves adverse employment decisions, such as reprimand or discharge of an employee, because the employee's wages have been garnished. The second concerns the use of consumer credit reports.

Garnishment of employees' wages

A wage garnishment is the legal procedure by which a court orders earnings withheld from an employee's wages in order to satisfy an outstanding debt the employee owes to a party other than the employer. Wage garnishments are regulated at the federal level by the Consumer Credit Protection Act. In addition, many states have adopted their own, often stricter, laws concerning wage garnishments. Also, disciplining an employee because of garnishments may be unlawful discrimination under Title VII, on the theory that certain protected groups such as women and minorities accrue credit problems more often than do others.

Consumer Credit Protection Act
Purpose
The Consumer Credit Protection Act (CCPA) limits the amount of an individual's earnings that an employer may be required to withhold from the individual's wages in order to pay off any one debt.

Applicability to employers
The CCPA applies to employers in all fifty states, the District of Columbia, Puerto Rico, and all other U.S. territories.

Prohibited employment decisions based on garnishment of wages

Under the CCPA, it is unlawful for an employer to discharge or take other adverse action against an employee because the employee's wages have been subjected to garnishment for any **one** indebtedness. "One indebtedness" is the amount found owing and ordered paid as the result of a legal proceeding, and may include debts owed to **one or more** creditors. Because the CCPA forbids termination only for "one indebtedness," an employer may lawfully discharge an employee after having to garnish the employee's wages because of a **second** indebtedness. However, the second garnishment must actually take place before termination is lawful. An employer may not discipline an employee if it merely receives a notice to garnish wages, but the wages are never actually withheld.

"Levies" versus "garnishments"

The protection against discharge is for any **one** garnishment proceeding. In a typical situation, the amount determined due by a court is not withheld from an employee's wages in one lump sum, but rather withdrawn in smaller portions or "levies" over an extended period of time. Therefore, multiple levies made against an employee's wages in satisfaction of that one proceeding do not constitute a separate "garnishment" each time they are made; rather, they are merely a portion of the single garnishment. This principle applies regardless of the number of creditors who seek satisfaction by means of that one proceeding. In other words, as the result of one garnishment proceeding, an individual could owe several creditors, but it would still be considered a single garnishment.

Employer reprimands based on first garnishment

Reprimands given to employees by an employer for a "first-time" garnishment pursuant to a progressive discipline policy cannot be counted toward termination. That is, if the employee's wages are garnished for the first time, the employer cannot use this garnishment as a basis for issuing a first warning under a progressive discipline system. Instead, the employer must wait until the employee's wages are garnished for a second time before taking disciplinary steps that may lead to further discipline, including termination.

Lapse of time between garnishments

When a significant amount of time has lapsed between a first and second garnishment, it may be unlawful to discharge an employee because of the second garnishment. As a general rule, termination based on garnishments separated by a year or more will be carefully scrutinized by a court.

Protection renewed with each new job

The CCPA's protection against termination is renewed with each new position; garnishments from previous jobs do not "follow" the individual.

Penalties for violations

Employees who are unlawfully disciplined may be entitled to reinstatement and/or back pay. An employer who willfully violates the provisions of the CCPA may also be fined or imprisoned up to one year, or both. The Department of Labor's Wage Hour Division is the federal agency responsible for administering and enforcing the CCPA.

State regulations

The CCPA specifically permits states to enact laws restricting the garnishment of wages, but only to the extent that they are "substantially similar" to the provisions contained in the CCPA. For a summary of individual state laws, refer to pages 200-205. All of the states that have enacted wage garnishment statutes place restrictions on discharge, and many also place restrictions on reprimands.

Special rules for child support garnishment

Employers should note that some states, for example, Iowa and South Dakota, make it a criminal act to discharge or refuse to hire an individual because that individual's income is or will be subject to garnishment for child support. Other states, such as Louisiana and New York, hold an employer in contempt of court for such conduct.

Title VII of the Civil Rights Act

Title VII applies to all employers with 15 or more employees, and includes labor organizations and employment agencies in its definition of "employer."

Prohibited employment decisions based on garnishment of wages

Because women and minorities are perceived as being subjected to wage garnishments more often than others, a policy of disciplining employees for wage garnishments may have a disparate impact on these protected groups. Even if such a policy is found to adversely affect minorities, an employer may avoid liability if it has a legitimate business reason for having the policy. While there is no clear definition of a "legitimate business necessity," factors courts have considered include:

- inconvenience to an employer in handling paperwork

- negative community relations when employees fail to pay just debts

- garnishments as evidence of general employee irresponsibility.

It is clear, however, that at a minimum, the policy must be shown to be "related to job performance" or necessary to "measure job capability."

Penalties for violations

Penalties are the same as for all other Title VII violations that are based on disparate impact.

Suggestions for compliance
Address policies concerning wage garnishments in employee handbook

Employers who discipline employees for excessive garnishments should have a written policy. Be sure to include the policy in the employee handbook and clearly inform employees that excessive garnishments may lead to disciplinary action up to and including termination.

Base employment decisions on non-discriminatory factors

Most employment decisions do not require consideration of an individual's credit history. Unless necessary for a legitimate and compelling business reason (for example, positions that involve handling large sums of money, employment decisions should be made without reference to an applicant's or employee's credit history).

Use of applicants' credit history

A "consumer credit report" is a compilation of personal information relating to an individual's credit history, character, general reputation, personal characteristics or mode of living, gathered by reporting agencies who are in the business of supplying such information to third parties, such as employers, for a fee.

An "investigative consumer report" is a consumer credit report in which the reporting agency compiles the personal information relating to an individual's credit history, character, general reputation, personal characteristics or mode of living through personal interviews with the individual's neighbors, friends, associates and acquaintances.

The Fair Credit Reporting Act (FCRA) is the federal law that regulates the preparation and dissemination of consumer credit reports by reporting agencies and their use by employers for employment-related purposes. Although employers are allowed to request and utilize credit reports, the impact of the FCRA on individual employee rights, and potential liability if not used within the bounds of the law, are important considerations for employers to keep in mind. Many states have also adopted laws that restrict employers' use of credit reports. Moreover, using credit reports may be unlawful discrimination under Title VII.

Fair Credit Reporting Act

The Fair Credit Reporting Act, which is actually a part of the Consumer Credit Protection Act, was enacted in order to restrict the wide availability of consumer reports, to regulate reporting agency standards, and to provide the consumer with an opportunity to refute inaccuracies.

Applicability to employers

The FCRA applies to employers in all 50 states, the District of Columbia, Puerto Rico, and all other U.S. territories.

Prohibited employment decisions based on consumer reports

The FCRA allows employers to use consumer credit reports for "employment purposes," which include the consideration or evaluation of an individual for employment, promotion, reassignment, or retention by an employer. However, any other use is strictly prohibited and unlawful. Moreover, even if an employer utilizes the report for a legitimate employment purpose, the employer may still face liability if the notification requirements are not met.

Notification requirements

An employer who obtains a credit report on an applicant must notify the applicant in a clear and conspicuous written disclosure that a credit report will be used as part of the application process. Employers are required to obtain written consent from the applicant before a credit report may be obtained. Employers must also confirm to the reporting agency that the employer has and will comply with all notification and reporting requirements to the applicant. A sample employer credit report request and a sample employee authorization to obtain a credit report appear at the end of this chapter.

An employer who relies on a consumer credit report either in whole or in part in denying employment to an applicant is required to disclose this fact to the applicant as well as the identity of the reporting agency from which the report was received.

The employer must also notify the applicant that he or she has a right to obtain a free copy of the consumer report from the reporting agency, and that he or she has a right to dispute the accuracy or completeness of any information in the consumer report with the reporting agency.

Employer's right to request report ceases when employment does

An employer should be aware that once an employee has resigned from employment, the employer no longer has a right under FCRA to obtain a consumer credit report on that employee. This is true even if an employer suspects an employee of misconduct such as embezzling funds.

If a credit report is obtained, maintain confidentiality

If an employer obtains a credit report on an applicant and the applicant is hired by the employer, the credit report must be kept confidential. Further, employers should not rely on the report in making subsequent employment decisions unless compelled by business necessity.

Penalties for violations

Under FCRA, both civil and criminal penalties may be imposed for violations. Violators may be held liable for actual damages, attorney's fees, and all court costs. In addition, willful violators can be held liable for punitive damages. The Federal Trade Commission has the authority to enforce FCRA, except where provided otherwise by federal law.

State regulations

FCRA permits states to further regulate the use of consumer credit reports. Many states that have adopted their own statutes also impose strict requirements concerning notification of a prospective or current employee when an inquiry is made into that individual's consumer credit history. For a summary of individual state laws, refer to pages 200-205. Like FCRA, several states require employers to notify applicants if a credit report will be used **for any purpose at all**, rather than merely if it is relied upon to deny employment.

Title VII of the Civil Rights Act

The basic parameters of Title VII outlined above in the discussion of wage garnishments also apply to disparate impact claims based on employer use of consumer credit reports.

Employment decisions based on consumer reports

Because Title VII prohibits an employer from utilizing policies or practices that have a disparate impact on persons in one or more of its protected classes, a discrimination claim may exist where an employer relies on credit reports in making employment decisions (for example, hiring, promotion, termination), and the ultimate result is that members of a protected group, such as women and minorities, are denied employment in a disproportionate number to those outside the protected group.

Employer's defense of business necessity

Just as business necessity may shield an employer from liability in the wage garnishment context, it is also a limited defense justifying the use of consumer credit reports. Again, the "business necessity" must be sufficiently job-related. This defense has been the most successful in the banking industry, where it can be argued that a person with a credit problem might be tempted to steal money.

Penalties for violations

Penalties are the same as for all other Title VII violations that are based on disparate impact.

Suggestions for compliance
Know the applicable federal and state laws

Ensure that your actions comply with both federal and state law, and be aware of any inconsistencies between the two that require special attention.

Only request report if truly necessary to make an employment decision

Always make sure you have a legitimate business reason for requesting an individual's consumer credit report.

Obtain applicant's consent first

Always require applicants to sign a consent form allowing you to request a consumer credit report. Be cautious, however, because even if consent is obtained, the manner in which credit information may be used in the hiring process is still limited by FCRA as well as any related state law.

If report is used to deny employment, notify applicant

FCRA requires you to provide the applicant with the name, address, and telephone number of the agency from which you obtained the credit report. This disclosure may be made orally, in writing or electronically.

Commonly asked questions and answers

Q. What is subject to garnishment under the CCPA?

A. Wage garnishments can be applied to all individuals who receive personal earnings. Garnishment restrictions do not apply to bankruptcy court orders or debts due for federal and state taxes.

Q. Can the term "one indebtedness" refer to a debt owed to more than one creditor?

A. Yes. The term refers to a single garnishment proceeding, that is, a lawsuit or administrative action, regardless of the number of creditors seeking satisfaction from that one proceeding.

Q. May an employer issue a warning to an employee as a result of a first time garnishment?

A. Yes, the warning is permissible if given under an established employment policy or practice. However, the warning may not count against the employee under any progressive discipline policy.

Q. Can an assignment of wages be considered a garnishment?

A. An assignment of wages is a private transaction in which an employee unilaterally and voluntarily transfers his right to collect his wages to a creditor, in order to satisfy a debt with that creditor. The CCPA, however, considers "garnishment" to mean a legal proceeding that results in requiring an individual's earnings to be withheld by an employer to satisfy the individual's debt to a creditor. Consequently, an assignment of wages is not considered a garnishment because it does not fall within the CCPA's definition of a "garnishment."

Q. Because the CCPA protects against discharge because of "one indebtedness," can an employee incur another debt with the same creditor or extend the original debt and still retain the same protection if additional garnishments are made in the future?

A. The law is not clear concerning "open" or "running" accounts. However, the term "one indebtedness" is defined in terms of one "judgment" or one garnishment proceeding. Therefore, it is likely that if the creditor seeks additional garnishments based on a separate debt or judgment, the CCPA would not protect the employee.

Q. Can an employer suspend an employee without pay for recurring garnishment proceedings resulting from a single indebtedness in an effort to persuade the employee to take more responsibility in meeting his or her obligations to creditors?

A. Generally, yes. However, employers should avoid these types of "morality" actions. If, for instance, the suspension is for an excessive or indefinite period of time so that the employee's return to work in unlikely, the suspension may be considered equivalent to firing and will be construed as an unlawful discharge.

Q. What about a situation where an employee's wages are garnished by a single creditor the employee has the garnishment voluntarily released by the creditor, but the debt remains unpaid. Sometime later, the same creditor obtains a garnishment against the employee for the same debt. Does this constitute a second garnishment?

A. "One indebtedness" refers to a single debt, regardless of the number of levies made against it. Therefore, this does not constitute a second garnishment and the employer may not discharge the employee because of these successive levies against the single debt.

Q. What types of questions relate to an individual's "credit history?"

A. Anything concerning financial accounts, such as credit cards or bank accounts; property ownership, including things such as a home or car; whether the individual has ever declared bankruptcy, etc.

Q. Some employment agencies request information on their internal forms concerning home ownership, car ownership, bank accounts, and even the applicant's spouse's job or title. Is this discriminatory?

A. While an employment agency is not prohibited from asking such questions, if the information is relied upon in making an employment decision, this may be discriminatory unless there was a valid business reason necessitating reliance on the information.

Q. May an employer ask applicants whether or not they own a car since car ownership is an indication of reliability?

A. Although it may indicate reliability, such an inquiry is not permissible unless related to an essential function (other than regular attendance) of the job. For example, it would be appropriate to ask an individual applying for a floral delivery job where the drivers are required to use their own vehicles to make the deliveries whether or not he/she owns a car. However, employers may ask applicants if they are able to arrive regularly at the starting time, without asking how they will get to work.

Q. May an employer reject an applicant who refuses to provide written consent for the employer to obtain a consumer credit report?

A. Generally, yes. However, employers should have a legitimate business reason for obtaining a consumer credit report on job applicants. If an employer does have such a business reason, then the applicant's failure to provide written consent to the employer may be grounds not to hire the applicant.

	Wage garnishment regulations		State regulations on pre-employment use of consumer credit reports		
	Restrictions on reprimand*	Restrictions on discharge	Notification by employer required if denied employment	Notification required for other uses	Special notes
Alabama	No	Yes	No	No	
Alaska***	Yes	Yes	No	No	
Arizona***	Yes	Yes	Yes	Yes	
Arkansas	No	No	No	No	
California	No	Yes	Yes	Yes Must notify applicant within 3 days after requesting report unless being used for promotion, reassignment, or retention.	
Colorado	Yes***	Yes	No Administration regulations discourage pre-employment questions regarding economic status.	Yes Employee or applicant must be informed that a credit report may be requested – must consent in writing.	
Connecticut	Yes	Yes	No	No	
Delaware	No	Yes	No	No	
Dist of Columbia	Yes***	Yes	No	No	
Florida	Yes	Yes	No	No	
Georgia	No	Yes	No	No	
Hawaii	Yes	Yes	No	No	
Idaho	Yes***	Yes	No Administration regulations discourage pre-employment questions regarding economic status.	No	

	Wage garnishment regulations		State regulations on pre-employment use of consumer credit reports		
	Restrictions on reprimand*	Restrictions on discharge	Notification by employer required if denied employment	Notification required for other uses	Special notes
Illinois	Yes	Yes	No	No	
Indiana	No	Yes	No	No	
Iowa	Yes***	Yes	No	No	
Kansas	Yes***	Yes	Yes	Yes	Must be informed in writing that a report was requested and mailed to person within 3 days after report was first requested.
Kentucky	No	Yes	No	No	
Louisiana***	Yes	Yes	No	No	Applicant entitled to a copy of credit report if denied employment. Must request report in writing.
Maine	Yes***	Yes	Yes	Yes Denial of **any** benefit based on report must be disclosed.	
Maryland	No	Yes	Yes	Yes	Employer must disclose to consumer in writing that an investigative report may be made and mail it within 3 days of first request.
Massachusetts	Yes***	Yes	Yes	Yes If investigative report, employer must give written notice to employee or applicant.	Individual can request copy of report and identification of anyone supplied to within last 2 years.

	Wage garnishment regulations		State regulations on pre-employment use of consumer credit reports		
	Restrictions on reprimand*	Restrictions on discharge	Notification by employer required if denied employment	Notification required for other uses	Special notes
Michigan	Yes	Yes	No	No	Request for report must be authorized by employee in writing.
Minnesota	Yes	Yes	Yes	Yes	Notification required for **any** employment use; also must inform if requesting investigative report.
Mississippi***	Yes	Yes	No	No	
Missouri	Yes***	Yes	No Administration regulations discourage pre-employment questions regarding economic status.	No	
Montana	Yes***	Yes	Yes	Yes Must notify within 3 days of requesting an investigative report.	
Nebraska	Yes***	Yes	No	No	
Nevada	Yes	Yes	Yes	No	
New Hampshire	No	No	Yes	Yes If request investigative report, must disclose to individual.	Individual can request copy of report and identification of anyone supplied to within last 2 years.
New Jersey	Yes	Yes	Yes	Yes	Must be informed in writing that a credit report may be obtained and consumer authorizes in writing the procurement of a report.

	Wage garnishment regulations		State regulations on pre-employment use of consumer credit reports		
	Restrictions on reprimand*	Restrictions on discharge	Notification by employer required if denied employment	Notification required for other uses	Special notes
New Mexico	Yes	Yes	No	No	
New York	Yes	Yes	No	Yes For **any** use at all.	Individual can request copy of report and identification of anyone supplied to within last 2 years.
North Carolina	Yes**	Yes**	No	No	
North Dakota	Yes***	Yes	No	No	
Ohio	Yes***	Yes	No	No	
Oklahoma	Yes	Yes	No Upon request reporting agency must identify persons to whom report has been furnished for employment purposes within 2 years.	No	
Oregon	No	Yes	No	No	
Pennsylvania	Yes	Yes	No	No	
Rhode Island***	Yes	Yes	Yes	Yes	An employee must be informed that a credit report may be requested and supply name and address of credit bureau making the report.
South Carolina	Yes***	Yes	No	No	
South Dakota***	Yes	Yes	No	No	
Tennessee***	Yes	Yes	No	No	

	Wage garnishment regulations		**State regulations on pre-employment use of consumer credit reports**		
	Restrictions on reprimand*	Restrictions on discharge	Notification by employer required if denied employment	Notification required for other uses	Special notes
Texas	No	No	No	No	On request of consumer, the name of each person requesting credit information during preceding 6 months must be disclosed, along with the date of request.
Utah	Yes	Yes	No	No	
Vermont***	Yes	Yes	No	No	
Virginia	No	Yes	No	No	
Washington	Yes	Yes	Yes	Yes	Must disclose in writing that a report may be procured and, before taking any adverse action the employer must provide applicant or employee the name, address and telephone number of the reporting agency; the person's rights; and a reasonable opportunity to respond.
West Virginia	Yes	Yes	No Administrative regulations discourage pre-employment questions regarding economic status	No	

	Wage garnishment regulations		State regulations on pre-employment use of consumer credit reports		
	Restrictions on reprimand*	Restrictions on discharge	Notification by employer required if denied employment	Notification required for other uses	Special notes
Wisconsin	Yes	Yes	No Administrative regulations discourage pre-employment questions regarding economic status.	No	
Wyoming	Yes***	Yes	No	No	

* Refers to states that prohibit any reprimand or warning at all, even if part of a progressive disciplinary or termination policy, because of a wage garnishment due to a single indebtedness.

** For debt owed public hospitals only or for health care coverage.

*** For support provisions in a divorce.

Alaska also has restrictions it applies to student loans.

Request for consumer credit report

–SAMPLE–

Date_____

Consumer Reporting Agency

Address

To whom it may concern:

[Employer Name] requests a consumer credit report for [Applicant/Employee Name and other required information]. A signed authorization to obtain the consumer credit report is enclosed herewith. In addition, [Employer Name] confirms that it has and will comply with all notification and reporting requirements under the Fair Credit Reporting Act.

Please forward the consumer credit report to the attention of [Name] at [Employer Name and Address]. Questions can be directed to [Name/Title] at [Telephone Number].

_____

Sincerely,

[Name/Title]

Enclosure

Authorization to obtain consumer credit report

–SAMPLE–

I have been notified that [Employer Name] would like to obtain my consumer credit report in connection with my application for employment. I authorize [Employer Name] to obtain such a report and release [Employer Name] from any liability connected with obtaining such a report.

_____

Date

_____

Name of Applicant or Employee

_____

Signature of Applicant or Employee

Practical pointers

An employer **SHOULD**:

- Establish a wage garnishment warning-discharge policy separate from any general warning-discharge policy (such as for tardiness or misconduct). By keeping these policies separate, the employer will not risk unlawfully terminating an employee based in part on a garnishment due to a single indebtedness.

- Put any wage garnishment warning-discharge policy in writing, and include it an employee handbook. Be sure the policy clearly informs employees that more than one garnishment may lead to disciplinary action up to and including discharge.

- Be aware that some states have special rules regarding garnishment for child support and will impose stricter penalties for violations of those rules.

- Notify the applicant or employee, in writing, that the employer intends to use a credit report to determine his or her eligibility for employment, promotion, or termination.

- Obtain written authorization, including a brief explanation of the limited employment-related purpose for which the information will be used, from the applicant or employee whose credit report the employer intends to request from a reporting agency before doing so.

- Verify information received from a consumer credit reporting agency for accuracy. Employers who rely on errors contained in a credit report in making an employment decision can be held liable even though the incorrect information was obtained from a reporting agency.

- If information contained in a consumer credit report is relied upon in making an employment decision, the employer **should** document this internally and ensure its confidentiality. The employer also **must** notify the applicant or employee of such reliance and provide him or her with the name, address, and telephone number of the agency from whom the employer obtained the information. This notification may be given orally, in writing, or through electronic means.

Practical pointers

An employer **MAY NOT**:

- Terminate an employee based in whole or in part on a first-time garnishment.

- Terminate an employee because of his/her receipt of notice of a second garnishment where the wages have not yet been withheld from the employee's paycheck.

- Ask questions on an application form seeking information beyond what can be justified as necessary for legitimate business reasons. For example, a prudent employer should eliminate all questions concerning credit history, wage garnishment, bankruptcy, home and automobile ownership, spouse's occupation and job title, and similar matters from its standard application form.

- Obtain a credit report from a reporting agency unless the employer has certified to the reporting agency that it has and will comply with all notification and reporting requirements to the applicant or the employee.

- Retain credit information as part of an employee's personnel file. An employer should keep this information in an employee's personnel file only as long as business necessity requires. After the business necessity has expired, delete the information. This will diminish the risk of unlawful reliance on the information in the future for a reason that may not be considered a business necessity.

- Request a consumer credit report on a former employee, even if the employee is suspected of embezzling funds from either the employer or the employer's clients.

Glossary

If there are any other glossary terms that you think would be helpful, please call 800-848-5645.

arbitration

See page 31, **Mandatory arbitration** and **Survival Guide #6, Federal Employment Laws and Regulations**.

assignment of wages

A transfer by an employee of his/her right to collect wages to a creditor in order to satisfy a debt.

backpay

Accrued but uncollected wages. Backpay may be awarded to a prevailing plaintiff in an employment discrimination lawsuit.

bona fide occupational qualification

A qualification that is essential to carry out the responsibilities of a job.

burden of proof

Obligation to affirmatively prove a fact in a dispute.

collective bargaining

Negotiations between an employer and the recognized representative of the employer's employees for the purpose of entering into a contract concerning wages, hours and other conditions of employment.

compensatory damages

Compensation or indemnity awarded to a person to compensate for the actual loss suffered or injury sustained.

concerted activity

Activity carried out by two or more employees for mutual aid and protection or by a single employee exercising rights under a collective bargaining agreement or on behalf of a union.

consumer report

A report containing any oral, written or other communication of information by a "consumer reporting agency" relating to a consumer's credit history or standing, character, general reputation, personal characteristics or mode of living.

consumer reporting agency

Any individual or corporation which regularly engages in the practice of gathering information on consumer credit for the purpose of supplying it to third parties such as employers.

defamation

See **Survival Guide #6** or **Survival Guide #7**.

disability

Under the Americans with Disability Act, a disability is a physical or mental impairment that substantially limits one or more life activities. See page 88, **Disability defined**.

disparate impact

Using a neutral employment policy or practice that disproportionately impacts persons within a protected class as compared to persons outside the protected class.

disparate treatment

Treating an employee or applicant differently than others because of the person's protected status or conduct.

earnings

Compensation paid or payable for personal services, whether as wages, salary, commission, bonus or otherwise, including periodic payments pursuant to a pension or retirement plan.

essential job functions

A function is essential if:

- the job exists to accomplish the function

    or

- only a limited number of employees can perform the function

    or

- the function is highly specialized and an employee is hired for his or her expertise in the area.

federal contractor

A person, partnership or corporation doing business with the federal government, or a subcontractor.

frontpay

Future wages that an employee or applicant would have earned but for the employer's discriminatory actions. Frontpay may be awarded to a prevailing plaintiff in an employment discrimination lawsuit. Frontpay is measured from the time a judgment is rendered against an employer to some reasonable point in the future. See also page 209, **backpay**.

garnishment

Any legal or administrative procedure through which the earnings of an employee are required to be withheld by the employee's employer for payment of a debt owed to someone other than the employer.

grievance

A complaint filed under a collective bargaining agreement claiming that the agreement was violated.

hostile work environment sexual harassment

Hostile environment sexual harassment occurs when an employer creates or permits the existence of an atmosphere of sexually offensive conduct or speech so pervasive and offensive that a reasonable employee could not tolerate working under such conditions.

impairment

An abnormal physical or mental condition which causes or contributes to a disability. See page 88, **An impairment that substantially limits one or more major life activities**.

independent contractor

Persons who are self-employed or work for an entity unrelated to the employer who are paid a fee for a service.

interactive process

Communication between employer and applicant or employee to exchange information about that individual's need for a work-related accommodation of a disability. This process may also include communication with the applicant's or employee's doctor.

"one indebtedness"

The amount of debt determined as the result of one garnishment proceeding, for example, court or administrative hearing, and can include multiple levels involving more than one creditor.

position statement

An employer's initial written response to a discrimination charge setting forth the employer's position.

protected status

A characteristic that employers are prohibited from considering such as race, sex, age, national origin, religion, disability, etc. when making employment decisions. See page 9, **What is protected status?**

punitive damages

Compensation awarded as punishment for outrageous conduct or to deter future conduct.

quid pro quo harassment

Quid pro harassment occurs when an employment decision is conditioned upon the granting of sexual favors or where an employee is punished for refusing to grant sexual favors.

reasonable accommodation

A reasonable accommodation is a modification to a job, employment practice, or work environment that makes it possible for an applicant or employee with a disability to perform the functions of a job. See page 101, **Reasonable accommodation**.

relief

The benefit a party may receive from a court after proving his or her claim.

Section 7 rights

The rights conferred upon employees by the Labor Management Relations Act to organize and join unions, to collectively bargain, to engage in concerted activity and to refrain from all such activities.

sexual harassment

Unwelcome sexual advances, request for sexual favors and other verbal or physical conduct of a sexual nature when:

- submission to such conduct is made a term or condition of an individual's employment

  or

- submission or rejection of such conduct is used as the basis for employment decisions

  or

- the conduct has the purpose or effect of unreasonably interfering with an individual's work performance or creating an intimidating, hostile or offensive working environment.

undue hardship

An action that presents significant difficulty, disruption, or expense in relation to the size of the employer, its resources, and the nature of its operations, or would require violation of safety/health laws and regulations. See page 104, **Undue hardship**.

whistleblowing/whistleblower

Whistleblower protection laws generally prohibit employers from taking adverse actions against employees who in good faith report suspected violations of law to public authorities. See page 176, **Whistleblowing** and **Survival Guide #6, Federal Employment Laws and Regulations**.

Index

B

C

D

E

F

G

H

I

J

L

M

N

O

P

R

S

American Chamber of
ACCP
Commerce Publishers

SURVIVAL GUIDES

■ **Federal Employment Laws and Regulations –
How to Comply**
A complete employer's guide to more than 1,900 key
issues of interest to all sizes and types of employers.
This revised guide boasts 40 chapters of accurate, up-
to-date information to help you unravel today's
complex employment laws and issues. It is perfect
for small business owners, human resources
managers, personnel directors . . . in other words,
anyone who deals with the rapidly changing world of
employment laws and regulations. Highlights of the
updated 2001 edition include new chapters on
workforce diversity and investigating employee
complaints. Also, new sections covering privacy and
high technology in the workplace, performance
evaluations, telecommuting, the Fair Credit Reporting
Act, workplace violence and termination. With 2 new
chapters, and 36 updated and revised chapters, this
edition will provide the information and answers you
need. 650 pages; $89.

■ **Employment Discrimination –
An Employer's Guide**
A comprehensive compliance tool with plenty of plain
English information on sensitive issues. With all
chapters revised and updated, this edition will help
put a stop to time-wasting, budget-breaking lawsuits,
penalties, back pay, attorney's fees and bad press.
Highlights of the 2001 edition include new sections
on disability discrimination, sexual harassment,
discrimination in employee benefits, resolving
employee disputes and charges, EEOC investigations,
and discrimination based on safety activities. This
Survival Guides provides instant guidance and
information that helps you respond to problems with
confidence. 248 pages; $89.

■ **Wages and Hours – An Employer's Guide**
A detailed employer's guide to one of the most
misunderstood issues employers face. Highlights of
the 2001 edition include new sections on wages and
hours enforcement, child labor, state break
requirements, state overtime requirements, minimum
wage, meal periods, exempt vs. non-exempt
employees and wages and hours district offices.
230 pages; $89.

■ **ADA: 10 Steps to Compliance**
A thorough, step-by-step guide to help you determine
exactly what you need to do to comply with the ADA.
Highlights of the updated 2001 edition include new
information on ADA coverage, modifying your hiring
and pre-employment practices, revising personnel
policies, reasonable accommodation, determining
who is a qualified disabled person and ensuring your
compliance. 500 pages; $89.

■ **Unemployment Compensation –
A Cost You Can Cut**
An easy-to-understand, practical "how to" manager's
guide. Completely updated for 2001, with new
information on weekly benefit amounts, average
claim by state, unemployment insurance quality
control report and annual cost of unemployment tax
rate per FTE. 168 pages; $89.

■ **Human Resource Letter –
People, Pay and Performance Issues**
This monthly newsletter provides updates to all of the
books, providing information spanning a wide variety
of topics in the Human Resources arena. Each month,
you will receive up-to-date coverage of the laws and
regulations affecting your business. Best of all, if you
would like more in-depth information on a topic
covered in an issue, simply call the author of that
article on the toll-free number provided. As a bonus,
you will receive one FREE issue with your first year's
subscription. Let our experienced HR staff help guide
you through the complex issues all employers must
face. $160 *(Annual Subscription)*.

■ **Federal Compliance Posters**
For your convenience, we have combined 5 federal
notices that employers must post on 1 combination
poster (22"x34"). Includes EEOC, FMLA and
minimum wage. Why make all those phone calls
when we've done it for you? *Ensure your compliance
– order now.* $10.

These **Survival Guides** will save you time, money and misunderstandings.
If you don't agree, you are welcome to return them for a full refund.

To order, see accompanying order form.

Qty.	Publication	Price*	Total
	Federal Employment Laws and Regulations – How to Comply	$89	
	Employment Discrimination – An Employer's Guide	$89	
	Wages and Hours – An Employer's Guide	$89	
	ADA: 10 Steps to Compliance	$89	
	Unemployment Compensation – A Cost You Can Cut	$89	
	Human Resource Letter – People, Pay and Performance Issues	$160 (Annual Subscription)	
	Set(s) of the Federal Compliance Posters	$10	

	Subtotal:	
(If ordering poster(s) ONLY: $4.50 for first poster + $0.50 for each additional poster) —	Shipping/handling:	$12.00
	Total:	
	Purchase Order #: (Optional)	

To order, complete this form and:

- **call us toll-free at 800-848-5645**

- **fax to 773-594-0776**

Or, mail with check payable to:

American Chamber of Commerce Publishers
5515 N. Cumberland Ave., Suite 815
Chicago, IL 60656

Our Guarantee

If you are not completely satisfied with any of these publications, please return them for a prompt and unquestioned refund.

Name _____

Title _____

Company _____

Address _____

City _____ State _____ Zip _____

(_____) _____
Area Code   Phone   Fax

Number of Employees _____

Check Enclosed (Payable to: American   Bill Me
Chamber of Commerce Publishers)

Charge to my: AMEX   VISA   MasterCard

Signature _____

Card Number _____ Exp. Date: _____

E-mail _____

EDBK